EMMANUEL
The Man Who Is God
Volume One

Studies in Christology

Dr. Ken Chant

EMMANUEL

The Man Who Is God

Volume One

Studies in Christology

By Ken Chant

Copyright © 2013 Ken Chant

ISBN 978-1-61529-075-8

Vision Publishing
1672 Main Street E 109
Ramona, CA 92065
1 800-9-VISION
WWW.BOOKSBYVISION.COM

All rights reserved worldwide. No part of this book may be reproduced in any manner without the written permission of the author except in brief quotations embodied in critical articles or reviews.

A NOTE ON GENDER

It is unfortunate that the English language does not contain an adequate generic pronoun (especially in the singular number) that includes without bias both male and female. So "he, him, his, man, mankind," with their plurals, must do the work for both sexes. Accordingly, wherever it is appropriate to do so in the following pages, please include the feminine gender in the masculine, and vice versa.

FOOTNOTES

A work once fully referenced will thereafter be noted either by "ibid" or "op. cit."

Contents

PREFACE ALPHA AND OMEGA	7
CHAPTER ONE THE MAN FROM NAZARETH	15
CHAPTER TWO JESUS IN THE GOSPELS	37
CHAPTER THREE WHAT HIS MANHOOD MEANS	55
CHAPTER FOUR CHRIST – THE ETERNAL LOGOS	67
CHAPTER FIVE THE LORD FROM HEAVEN	81
CHAPTER SIX THE MAN WHO IS GOD	91
CHAPTER SEVEN THE POWER OF GOD	101
CHAPTER EIGHT THE GREAT "I AM"	113
CHAPTER NINE ALL THE PROPHETS	135
CHAPTER TEN THE PRE-EMINENT CHRIST	153
CHAPTER ELEVEN THE TRANSFORMING CHRIST	169
CHAPTER TWELVE THE GREATEST THING IN THE WORLD	185
ADDENDA CHILD PRODIGIES	199

ABBREVIATIONS

Abbreviations commonly used for the books of the Bible are

Genesis	Ge	Habakkuk	Hb
Exodus	Ex	Zephaniah	Zp
Leviticus	Le	Haggai	Hg
Numbers	Nu	Zechariah	Zc
Deuteronomy	De	Malachi	Mal
Joshua	Js		
Judges	Jg		
Ruth	Ru	Matthew	Mt
1 Samuel	1 Sa	Mark	Mk
2 Samuel	2 Sa	Luke	Lu
1 Kings	1 Kg	John	Jn
2 Kings	2 Kg	Acts	Ac
1 Chronicles	1 Ch	Romans	Ro
2 Chronicles	2 Ch	1 Corinthians	1 Co
Ezra	Ezr	2 Corinthians	2 Co
Nehemiah	Ne	Galatians	Ga
Esther	Es	Ephesians	Ep
Job	Jb	Philippians	Ph
Psalm	Ps	Colossians	Cl
Proverbs	Pr	1 Thessalonians	1 Th
Ecclesiastes	Ec	2 Thessalonians	2 Th
Song of Songs	Ca *	1 Timothy	1 Ti
Isaiah	Is	2 Timothy	2 Ti
Jeremiah	Je	Titus	Tit
Lamentations	La	Philemon	Phm
Ezekiel	Ez	Hebrews	He
Daniel	Da	James	Ja
Hosea	Ho	1 Peter	1 Pe
Joel	Jl	2 Peter	2 Pe
Amos	Am	1 John	1 Jn
Obadiah	Ob	2 John	2 Jn
Jonah	Jo	3 John	3 Jn
Micah	Mi	Jude	Ju
Nahum	Na	Revelation	Re

Ca is an abbreviation of *Canticles*, a derivative of the Latin name of the *Song of Solomon*, which is sometimes also called the *Song of Songs*.

Note: *scripture translations are my own unless otherwise noted.*

Religion is the first thing and the last thing, and until a man has found God, and been found by God, he begins at no beginning and works to no end. He may have his friendships, his partial loyalties, his scraps of honour. But all these things fall into place and life falls into place only with God. (H. G. Wells) [1]

How can plurality consist with unity, or unity with plurality? To examine the fact closely is rashness, to believe it is piety, to know it is life, and life eternal.
(St Bernard of Clairvaux) [2]

Jesus Christ will be Lord of all or he will not be Lord at all. (St Augustine of Hippo) [3]

We get no deeper into Christ than we allow him to get into us. (John H Jowett) [4]

Christ is the still point of the turning world.
(T. S. Eliot) [5]

---

[1] Mr Brittling Sees it Through; McMillan Publishers, New York; 1916; pg. 442.

[2] The Westminster Collection of Christian Quotations; compiled by Martin H. Manser; Westminster John Knox Press, Louisville, Kentucky; 2001.

[3] Ibid.

[4] The Friend on the Road and Other Studies in the Gospels: *The Joy of Christian Life*; ch. 56; pub. in 1922.

[5] Although Eliot uses the expression "the still point of the turning world" in his poetry, I have not been able to find the quote as it is given above, although it is often cited.

6

Preface

Alpha and Omega

> "The coming of Jesus into the world is the most stupendous event in human history ... whatever is truly admirable in the achievements of the succeeding centuries, in art and literature, in music and architecture, in the quest for knowledge, and in the pursuit of justice and brotherliness in human-relations, derives from that same event ... I cannot but see it as towering sublimely above all others." [6]

This book is an explanation of that "stupendous event." My prayer when I began to write it was that the Father would help me to present to you his Son, not as a lifeless doctrine, but as a living Saviour. I hope you will find in these pages a Person, not a polemic; a Reality, not a creed.

Another way to describe this book, would be to say that it is a commentary on the four great affirmations about Christ that John makes at the beginning of his gospel, where he declares Christ's

Eternity	"in the beginning was the Word"
Equality	"and the Word was with God."
Deity	"and the Word was God."

---

[6] Malcolm Muggeridge, <u>Jesus - The Man Who Lives</u>; Fontana/Collins, London, UK, 1975; pg.11.

Humanity   "and the Word became flesh."

In those four sayings there is almost a complete Christology!

But the problem I have had to struggle with on almost every page is to stay simple, and to stay related to life. It is so easy to yield to the temptation to become learned but quite unlively. Whether I have managed to defeat that temptation, I would not dare to say. You must decide for yourself. Still, my desire has been to stir your imagination and your emotions rather than merely to instruct your mind. Could there be anything more incongruous than a coldly intellectual discussion, void of fire, empty of dreams, about the Man of Nazareth, who strides with such energy and drama across the pages of the Bible?

Yet there is profound mystery, both in the gospel and in our personal experience of Christ, and any attempt to clarify this mystery must tread along difficult paths. I can only hope that I have handled scripture with proper reverence, while avoiding the kind of tortuous and abstruse writing I have found in many books on this subject.

THE LIMITS OF THEOLOGY

In the end, Jesus is a *person*, and we can come to know him only as we come to know any other person – by experiencing him in a close and continual relationship. How can you say that you know a man if you have done no more than read a scientific analysis of his heredity, genes, education, social status, and the like? Knowing *about* him, and actually knowing *him*, are not the same!

So the real Jesus cannot be found in the mists of philosophy, nor in the dogmas of theology. He must be found in life, or not at all. Penitential tears, the anguish of a lonely soul, a dream of endless glory, a sigh for heaven, will more swiftly bring one to Christ than all the convoluted arguments of learned divines.

Malcolm Muggeridge perceived this paradox when he wrote –

> Only mystics, clowns, and artists, in my experience, speak the truth, which, as Blake was always insisting, the imagination alone can grasp. Thus an animist grovelling naked in the African bush before painted stone may well be nearer to the heart of things than any Einstein or Bertrand Russell, and a painted circus clown riding a bicycle round and round a circus ring more attuned to the reality of life than a Talleyrand or a Bismarck can hope to be. Jesus was making the same point when he insisted that God has revealed to the foolish what is hidden from the wise. [7]

All theology should be an attempt to define some encounter people have had with God. When theology wanders away from experience and begins to deal with factless philosophy, it becomes vainglorious and ultimately useless. As Thomas Lindsay has somewhere written – "True theology will be aimed at expounding the faith of the pious believer, rather than at unfolding metaphysical mysteries."

Nonetheless, even a theology that refuses to separate itself from the way people actually experience God may still find, as Ezekiel did, that the waters of divine action and revelation refuse to remain always shallow. He who pursues the knowledge of God will soon find himself wading knee-deep,

---

[7] Ibid. pg. 38

and then up to his loins, and then in waters *"deep enough to swim in, a river that cannot be passed through!"* (47:5)

THE IMPORTANCE OF THEOLOGY

Attempts to cope with this flood (which springs out of any meeting between God and men and women) have led to the development of two kinds of theology:

<u>Dogmatic Theology</u> which attempts to build on the Biblical data in such a way as to clarify or define matters that are either not dealt with or are insufficiently defined in the Bible.

Many subjects in scripture either lack adequate definition, or are fully explained in some aspects, but not in others. *Dogmatic theology* is an attempt to fill up these empty places in the biblical revelation. Therefore *dogmatic theology* goes beyond scripture, but it should certainly not contradict nor alter scripture. Here are three important examples –

1. the doctrine of the *Trinity* (which is nowhere formally presented in scripture);
2. the doctrine of the *Last Things* (the various "eschatologies" produced by different teachers are dogmatic attempts to correlate the biblical data into a single scheme of events, past, present and future);
3. the doctrine of the *Church* (the various "ecclesiologies" are dogmatic attempts to build onto or into scripture a cohesive pattern of church structure and government).

Then there is **<u>Biblical Theology</u>**, which is primarily concerned with what the Bible actually says, and with Christian life and experience.

In contrast with dogmatic theology (which explores the realms of pure thought beyond the words of scripture, and is not much concerned with matters of personal experience), *biblical theology* confines itself mostly within the words of scripture, and is deeply concerned with individual Christian growth.

I hope you will find here a fair mixture of both kinds of theology. I am not timorous about venturing beyond scripture when the Bible gives only hints or disconnected pieces of information. But my final goal is ever only to illuminate scripture for you, and then to trust that this brighter light will result in a life transformed by a richer discovery of Christ.

Yet still I tremble, fearful lest I have been guilty of obscuring what should have been radiant, and thus placing myself under the scorn expressed 400 years ago by John Donne –

> In all religions as much care hath been
> Of temples' frames, and beauty, as rites within.
> As all which go to Rome, do not thereby
> Esteem religions, and hold fast the best,
> But serve discourse, and curiosity,
> With that which doth religion but invest,
> And shun th'entangling labyrinths of schools,
> And make it wit, to think the wiser fools ...
> (as nice thin school divinity
> Serves heresy to further or repress) ...
> Oft from new proofs, and new phrases,
>   new doubts grow,
> As strange attire aliens the men we know.

The poet plainly had a low opinion of the tortuous arguments of mediaeval Roman schoolmen, who were unable to assess the real value of religion, and were busy with religion's frame and ornament, instead of its inner heart. They were ever searching after curious matters for discourse, and thought it witty to turn wise men into fools.

Their discourses seemed weighty, but in Donne's view they were "thin", heavy only in irrelevancy, and could as well be used to create heresy as to destroy it. Their arguments so disguised the truth as to make it "alien" to those who once knew it, and from every new proof a new doubt arose!

Every page of this study is at risk of falling into the same morass. I can say only that I have striven to avoid twisting the truth either by undue complexity or naïve simplicity, and to portray truthfully the glory of the Saviour.

MY SOURCE AND MY REASONS

Before concluding this *Preface*, I must declare my debt to an unpublished manuscript on "Christology", written by my brother, Barry Chant, for use in the *House of Tabor* (Adelaide, South Australia). That college text provided the basic guideline for the structure of the following chapters. However, Barry would look in vain if he tried to find his original here, for I have expanded his outline study until scarcely any semblance of it remains. Where my text depends more directly upon Barry's study, acknowledgement is given in a footnote.

Finally, some explanation of the reason for this course. All debate about Jesus our Lord, where he came from, who he is, eventually comes to three matters –

- Some deny either that Jesus was human, or that he was divine.

- Others, who allow that he was both human and divine, still question either the fulness of his humanity or the fulness of his deity.

- And there are those who deny that the two natures were united in one person, saying either that he had two natures and was two persons, or that his two natures were mingled together so as to form a new third nature.

Orthodox belief, which fills the following pages, [8] argues that we dare not sacrifice the humanity of Christ to his deity, nor his deity to his humanity; nor may we merge deity and humanity together to form a new hybrid nature, neither divine nor human; and we dare not divide Christ into more than one person.

There is but one Saviour, Jesus, and in him, the God-man, lies all our hope of eternal life and of inheritance in the kingdom of God.

---

[8] Not because it is "orthodox", but because I am persuaded of its essential truth. *If I become convinced that some commonly held dogma is wrong, then I don't hesitate to say so.

Chapter One

THE MAN FROM NAZARETH

There has appeared in our time, in Judea, a man of singular virtue, whose name is Jesus Christ, whom the barbarians esteem a prophet, but his followers love and adore him as an offspring of the immortal gods. He calls back the dead from the graves and heals all sorts of diseases with a word or a mere touch.

He is a tall man and well-shaped, of an amiable and reverend aspect, which they who look upon him both love and fear. His hair is of a colour that can hardly be described, almost wine-coloured, rich, and falling in waves about his shoulders, with a parting in the middle after the style of the Nazarenes. His forehead is high, imposing, and serene; his face free of any spot or wrinkle; his cheeks aglow with a delicate flush.

His nose and mouth are formed with exquisite symmetry; his beard is abundant, of a colour suitable to his hair, and divides below the chin, although it is not unduly long. His eyes are bright blue, clear and serene, conveying an innocent look, yet dignified, manly, and mature. In proportion of body he is most perfect and captivating, his hands and arms most delectable to behold.

He rebukes with terrible majesty, but in counsel he is mild and loving; he is cheerful, yet withal his address remains eloquent and grave, his dignity always unimpaired. Although his manner is exceedingly pleasant, no man has seen him laugh; but he has often wept in the presence of men. He is temperate, modest, and wise; a man, for his extraordinary beauty and divine perfections, surpassing in every sense the children of men.

Many years ago someone gave me the above description of Jesus. It was carelessly typed on a single sheet of paper, and with many errors, which I have corrected as well as I can. A sentence attached to the description claimed that it was *"composed by Publius Lentulus, Governor of Judea, and addressed to Tiberius Caesar, Emperor of Rome,"* and that it was found, carved in Aramaic on stone, in an excavated (but un-named) city.

Before I tell you whether or not the description is genuine, let me say that my reaction when I first read it was joy. At last! A clear image of my Saviour! A splendid image. A man's image. The image of a hero. A Christ to admire in his vibrant masculinity, his flawless features, his perfect stature, his admirable character, his serene confidence.

But that pleasure was brief, and soon supplanted by doubt. Somehow, the description lacked the sound of truth. The historical details were highly questionable, and the picture seemed to have little concurrence with the Jesus of Nazareth described in the gospels and in the prophets.

So I began to research the matter further, and was not surprised to find that the document was a forgery. There was indeed in Judea in the time of Tiberius a Roman official whose name was Lentulus. But the document ascribed to him, which is known to historians as *The Epistle of Lentulus*, is certainly spurious.

The date of the letter is unknown, but it was probably written in Italy sometime after the 13th century, and in its earliest forms it was reputed to have been copied from ancient Roman annals. Only later was it ascribed to Lentulus.

I am not sure how accurate my copy of the epistle is. I suspect that it may diverge considerably from the original. But it will serve as a useful introduction to this chapter. For it does show a common error in the way people, almost from the first century, have thought about Jesus.

They cannot usually deny that he was a man (although, as we shall see later, some have rejected his true humanity); yet still they are unwilling to allow him to be *just* a man. So, in one way or another, they add to his human nature some larger-than-life, or non-human, dimension. The *Epistle of Lentulus* is a prime example of this, but there have been many other similar attempts – especially by authors who have attributed to Jesus more miracles and spectacular deeds than the gospels record. Some of these are mentioned a few paragraphs below.

All those attempts to enlarge the gospel picture of Jesus probably stem from one of two things – either a desire to magnify his divine origin (that is, his deity) at the expense of his humanity; or else, an ascetic dislike for the human body, and a desire to remove Jesus as far as possible from being a normal man.

Now, in the next chapter (and in the second volume of this study) I will be writing about the limitless glory that does belong to Christ, and I will show you how scripture ascribes to him as much magnificence as anyone could yearn for him to possess. But before the *deity* of Jesus can be understood, his true *humanity* must be reckoned with.

JESUS THE MAN

Just what *did* Jesus look like?

We truly do not know. But I can tell you how to arrive at an approximation of his appearance. Go down to a busy shopping centre and look out for any young man, about 30 years of age, of average size and appearance. Ignore anyone who has an unusually strong physique, or is uncommonly handsome, or has a commanding aspect of authority, a kind of powerful "presence", a kingly mien. None of those things would have been characteristic of Jesus of Nazareth.

The earliest drawings that might help us, of which some 200 are still extant, date from the beginning of the 2nd century, and mostly follow the idea of the Good Shepherd, with the Shepherd portrayed as a young man – beardless, [9] bareheaded, wearing a peasant's tunic, usually sleeveless, sometimes with an added cloak thrown across his shoulder, and having about him an air of gentle, benign dignity.

Eusebius (Bk 7.18) describes a statue of Christ he had seen, which he said had been erected by Veronica, the woman Jesus healed of an issue of blood. It portrayed a fine-looking man, clad in a long robe, and bore the inscription, *To the Saviour and Benefactor*. [10]

---

[9] All the most ancient portraits of Jesus, in art and sculpture alike, show him beardless.

[10] Many scholars argue that it was actually a statue of an emperor, and the woman was a supplicant city or province; but others wonder how Eusebius could have mistaken such a familiar subject, or, if it was plainly a pagan statue, why the emperor Julian the Apostate took such pains to destroy it. (Julian was the nephew of Constantine the *Great*. He tried to restore the ancient myths and to turn the Roman Empire back to pagan worship, but after only a
– continued on next page

From infancy to manhood Jesus' development followed the usual human pattern; he evidently did not differ noticeably from his young playmates, except that he was well liked by all who knew him (Lu 2:52). His neighbours noticed that he was an exceptionally intelligent boy, wise beyond his years (verse 40); yet he was still obliged to grow in understanding and to learn by enquiry (verse 42). Certainly, there was nothing obviously supernatural about him; indeed, many children have shown far greater precocity than Jesus ever publicly displayed.[11] It is probable that almost any modern primary school child would know more about the world than Jesus could possibly have learned.

He did not possess either intuitive or acquired knowledge that was beyond attainment by normal human faculties; he did not possess the kind of instinctive and perfect knowledge that would be natural to a deity who was not hampered by human nature.

So, as the outside world saw Jesus, he was a normal, average man; in some respects perhaps the most "average" man who has ever lived. From another aspect, of course, Jesus was the most *uncommon* man who has ever lived, and much of this book will be devoted to describing his uniqueness and splendour. But before we discuss the things that were special about the Lord and his ministry, it is important to meet him where the scriptures first meet him, that is, in his true and ordinary humanity. If you do not *truly* meet him as *Jesus of*

---

couple of years on the throne he was mortally wounded in battle in 362, and his last words are said to have been, "Vicisti Galilaiee!" – "O Galilean, thou hast triumphed!" The 5th century church historian Sozomen tells the story of Julian's attempt to destroy the statue of Christ. See the *Addendum*, "Veronica's Statue of Christ."

(11)   See the *Addendum* on "Child Prodigies".

Nazareth, you will never fully understand him as the *Christ of Glory*. You must know him as the *Son of Man* before you can properly adore him as the *Son of God*.

A UNIQUE SAVIOUR

The idea of a Saviour who has come down to earth from heaven is not unique to Christianity. Many other great religions have believed in various kinds of divine incarnations, or theophanies. But Christianity is unique in its claim that the Saviour, though he came from heaven, was nonetheless fully human. Every other deity who is supposed to have appeared among men has been clothed with a spurious or artificial humanity. Their apparently "human" form was only a disguise, a temporary camouflage. They were pseudo humans. Their humanity was a pretence.

A clear example of this can be seen in the life of the Hindu deity Krishna. Most Hindus think of Krishna as a rather minor deity, a lesser expression of the great god Vishnu. But the *Hare Krishna* movement elevated Krishna to a place of supreme honour in its pantheon. The sect had its origins in Bengal, where in February 1486 a boy was born who came to be known as the Lord Caitanya Mahaprabhu. His followers worshipped him as an incarnation of Krishna. He himself claimed that Krishna was the Supreme Deity, and that this truth was revealed in two portions of the sacred Hindu Vedic writings – the *Srimad Bhagavatam*, and the *Bhagavad Gita*. For 500 years the movement was confined largely to India, but in recent years it has enjoyed remarkable expansion worldwide.

My copy of the *Srimad Bhagavatam* [12] contains an account of Caitanya's life, and includes a number of incidents that are supposed to show he was not merely a man, but actually an incarnate god. Notice, though, the contrast, when Caitanya and Jesus are put side by side –

CAITANYA	JESUS
In the *Bhagavad-Gita*, Lord Sri Krishna is depicted as "the Absolute Personality of Godhead, and his last teachings instruct that one should give up all modes of religious activities and accept him (Lord Sri Krishna) as the only worshipful Lord." "Lord Sri Caitanya ... is the self same Lord Sri Krishna. This time, however, he appeared as a great devotee of the Lord in order to preach about ... Krishna, the primeval Lord and the Cause of all causes" (page 18).	Notice that Krishna is said to be the supreme deity, and that Caitanya was an incarnation of Krishna, who was born into a human family in order to proclaim to the world his own true glory, and to claim the worship of all people. The parallel with the gospel story is obvious except there is no suggestion of a "Virgin Birth".
"The simultaneous occurrence of the Lord's appearance and the lunar	There is a resemblance here to the gospel story of the Christmas Star – a sign that

---

[12] Srimad Bhagavatam, First Canto, Part One; translation and commentary by A.C. Bhaktivedanta Swami Prabhupada; published 1970 by the International Society for Krishna Consciousness, New York. The page numbers shown refer to this edition.

eclipse indicated the distinctive mission of the Lord. This mission was to preach the importance of chanting the holy names of the Lord in this age of Kali (quarrel)" (page 10) "When the Lord was on the lap of his mother, he would at once stop crying as soon as the ladies surrounding him chanted the holy names and clapped their hands. This peculiar incident was observed by the neighbours with awe and veneration. Sometimes the young girls took pleasure in making the Lord cry and then stopping him by chanting the holy names ... When he was a mere baby crawling in the yard, one day a snake appeared before him, and the Lord began to play with it. All the members of the house were struck with fear and awe, but after a little while the snake went away ..."	the Child born was in some way unique. But the "mission" is certainly different – Caitanya will bring salvation through a repetitious litany, but Christ through fulfilling the holy law of God. These stories about Caitanya's childhood are not unlike those that have been told about other supposed incarnations of various deities. There is a universal opinion that if a god comes down to earth in human form, he will reveal his true identity by various prodigies, signs, or miracles.
"There are many similar incidences in his childhood. As a naughty boy he sometimes used to tease the orthodox brahamanas who used to bathe in the Ganges.	The gospels are remarkable for their insistence that Jesus wrought no miracle for its own sake, nor by his own unaided power (he said that his mighty works were

When the brahamanas complained to his father that he was splashing them with water instead of going to school, the Lord suddenly appeared before his father as though just coming from school with all his school clothes and books" (pages 10-12).	all done by the power of the Holy Spirit). Apart from what God the Father wrought through him, Jesus remained a normal man in his abilities and daily activities.

This absence of freak miracles in the life of Jesus, this dissimilarity of the gospels to other writings, and their refusal to pander to the human hunger for prodigies, has always been scandalous to a certain group of people. So various attempts have been made to rectify this "shortcoming" by supplying various supernatural feats that Jesus is supposed to have done, both as a child and as a man. For example, a set of documents called the *Apocryphal Gospels*, written during the early centuries of the church, provides a good source of such fictitious stories about Jesus –

> The silence and restraint of the canonical gospels ... are best appreciated when viewed against the background which the apocryphal gospels supply. Perhaps the most valuable service that the latter writings render is that comparison with them so strongly brings out the intrinsic value and superiority of our canonical gospels. They show us conclusively what men with a free hand could and would do.

> This is conspicuously the case with reference to the early years of Jesus. The extravagant and miraculous stories told concerning his infancy and childhood, taken by themselves, would suffice to crush out the historicity of Jesus and

consign him to the region of the mythical ... (We find a) congeries of grotesque wonder-tales concerning the doings of the Boy.

His miraculous powers proved to be of singular advantage to Joseph, for when a beam or plank has been cut too short, Jesus rectifies the mistake by merely pulling it out to the required length. He changes boys into kids and anon restores them to their former condition ... When playing with other boys and making figures of various beasts and birds, Jesus makes those he had formed walk and fly, eat and drink.

Wonderful works of healing are also ascribed to the Child ... for example ... a boy is near to death through having been bitten by a serpent. Jesus makes the serpent itself come and suck out all the poison from the wound; then he curses it and immediately the creature bursts asunder. The cure of demoniacs, of lepers, of the blind and maimed and sick, and the raising of the dead, are all ascribed to the child Jesus. [13]

Here are some further contrasts between Christ and Caitanya —

---

[13] <u>Dictionary of the New Testament</u>, Vol. I, "Christ and the Gospels;" edited by James Hastings; reprinted by Baker Book House, Grand Rapids, Michigan, 1973; pg. 298,299.

CAITANYA	JESUS
The story of Caitanya continues with a debate between him and "a champion scholar", in which the scholar was humiliated, while Caitanya (who was still a boy) showed astonishing erudition, prodigious feats of memory, and skill in exposing the errors of the pundit (pages 12-13).	Such incidents reveal a continued wish to separate the incarnate deity from ordinary humanity. The devotees of Caitanya cannot allow him to be limited to the attributes of a man, but the attributes of a god must be apparent in him to every onlooker. There is a sharp contrast here with the story Luke gives of the boy Jesus, 12 years old, earnestly learning at the feet of the doctors in the temple. They were amazed that one so young should display such an unusual thirst for knowledge, and should show such perception in the things of God. But there is no supernatural element in Luke's story. Jesus' understanding was certainly no more than could be expected of a youth whose mind was free of the corruption of sin, and whose heart was in sincere, untainted fellowship with God. But that reverend and lovely scene did not suit the apocryphal writers, who were determined that Jesus'

> humanity should be shattered by manifestations of divine anger, relentless strength, and superhuman knowledge.

Hence, strangest thing of all, a series of vindictive and destructive miracles are described which offer the most flagrant contrast to what we know of our Lord, and which, if true, would have made him a veritable terror to all with whom he came into contact. Boys who thwart him are immediately struck dead; others who take action against him are blinded.

> It is true that the mischief is usually repaired by him in response to earnest entreaty, but the vengeful malevolence is conspicuous throughout. In the stories, again, relating to his early education, Jesus is represented as being an "enfant terrible" to more than one master ... We find him represented as not only getting the upper hand of the great Rabbis in relation to the knowledge of the Torah, but as giving profound instruction to philosophers in astronomy, natural science, and medicine, explaining to them "physics, metaphysics, hyperphysics, and hypophysics", and many other things. [14]

---

[14] Ibid. page 299. The apocryphal gospels referred to are the "Childhood Gospel of Thomas", the "Arabic Gospel of the Childhood", and the "Gospel of Pseudo-Matthew", etc. See <u>The Ante-Nicene Nicene Fathers</u> Vol 8, Eerdmanns Pub. Co, Grand
– continued on next page

How far removed all those apocryphal inventions are from the simple and natural beauty of the gospels!

The story of Caitanya continues –

CAITANYA	JESUS
Caitanya could at times act quite vindictively – the story tells about him striking his maternal uncles with leprosy, barely being restrained from killing an unbeliever, driving a young devotee to suicide, and the like. These acts are all reckoned to be displays of divine wrath, and to be proof of his deity. (Pages 14,16,32.)	There have been many attempts, some open, some subtle, to posit the same thing of Christ – that is, there was something false, unreal, or preternatural about his human appearance. He was not truly a man. He did not really experience the range of human emotions, desires, frailties, limitations, hurts, hungers, and the like. His humanity was a similitude. We must reject all such folly as unscriptural nonsense.
"During his householder life, the Lord did not display many of the miracles which are generally expected from such personalities; but he did (perform some miracles) (page 16) ... Once when 16 years old, Caitanya walked	Notice the idea expressed about Caitanya, that "miracles are generally expected" from incarnate deities – yet not the kind of selfless miracles attributed to Jesus in the gospels; but rather, miracles whose

Rapids, 1979 reprint; pg. 376/18,20; 380/33,34,38; 396/9-13; 398/2-5; 400/1; 413/42. See also the Index volume (Vol 9), pg. 173, column c.

along a river bank with his father. He was naked, his father was clothed. Some beautiful young girls who were bathing naked, quickly covered themselves when the father passed by, although he was clothed, but did not do so when the youth passed by, though he was naked. The young ladies, when asked why, replied that Caitanya 'was purified, and when looking at them made no distinction between male and female' ... (he) was transcendental to sex relations (and) appeared very innocent (page 195,196).

"It is important to note that the Lord exhibited his divinity even from the lap of his mother, that his deeds are all superhuman (he lifted Govardhana Hill at the age of six) and that all these acts definitely prove him to be actually the Supreme Personality of the Godhead. Yet, due to his mystic covering, he was always accepted as an ordinary human child ... As such, the sages ... describe him as apparently resembling a human being, but actually he is the Supreme Almighty primary intent is to tell the world that the man who works them is no man at all, but actually a god in human clothing. Caitanya's humanity is artificial. Hence the girls were not embarrassed by the naked Caitanya, for they sensed he was not really a man, and had no sexual desire toward them. His human appearance was only "a mystic cover"; he "resembled" a human being, but he was actually a god – indeed the "Supreme God" Krishna pretending to be a man.

Personality of Godhead" (page 78). [15]

Our task therefore, prior to exploring the *divine* identity of Christ (which he does indeed possess), will be to examine the reality and ramifications of his true and real *human* nature.

We must demonstrate that Jesus was not a god in disguise. His human nature was not a mere camouflage. He was not a divine actor dressed in a human costume. His masculinity and sexuality were not pretence. He was indeed a true man.

But before beginning that quest, notice how the story of Tobit provides another illustration of how readily people are able to imagine a divine being camouflaged in a spurious human form. When the time came for the angel Raphael to reveal his true identity to Tobit, he apologised for the fact that his human shape and behaviour had been deceptive – *"You thought you saw me eating, but that was appearance and no more"* (Tobit 12:19). So, there were many early Christians who preferred to think the same thing about Jesus. They felt his glory would be diminished if it were claimed that food was necessary for him.

---

[15] I expect it will be obvious to you that I have been rather arbitrary in my choice of incidents from the life of Caitanya. I have ignored the teachings of the Krishna movement, many of which are noble, and I have ignored the many ordinary things, and the many fine things Caitanya is said to have done. I wanted only to draw attention to the claims of his devotees that his identity as an incarnate god can be established by certain non-human factors that are attributed to him. The writers of the apocryphal gospels attempted to do the same for Jesus. But the canonical gospels are remarkable for their insistence upon the true and regular humanity of Jesus.

In a similar manner, the *Koran* (Sura 5:113) refers to the legendary deeds of Christ – "Behold, thou makest out of clay, as it were, the figure of a bird;" and Muslim folk-lore contains many other fantastic tales about Jesus (whom Muslims number among the prophets).

Such stories show again the kind of Christ people would like to create, if they were not restrained by the four gospels. Here are two further examples from the Koranic stories about the childhood of Jesus –

> When the days of her confinement drew near, Mary was told to go to Bethlehem, lest her people should injure the child. Mary and Joseph went, under the guidance of Gabriel. The pangs of childbirth coming on, she got off her riding animal and rested under a date tree. Then Christ was born. Immediately a spring appeared and angels bathed the child.
>
> It is said that Jesus then said to his mother, "Do not sorrow, God has provided this fountain" ... (When) the Jews found her and the child under the tree, they began to make a tumult and reproached her ... She replied – "I am fasting today, whatever you want to know, ask the child."
>
> They became very angry, and said – "How shall we speak to the infant?" However, they asked him the circumstances of his birth. He said – "I am the slave of God, appointed to be a prophet and a blessing in whatever place I may be ... from the day of my birth to the day of my resurrection to life again." Having said this, he did not speak again till the natural time for an infant to speak arrived ...

Then Mary went to Jerusalem, where, seeing the miracles done by the child, people sought to destroy him ... (So Mary) went with Joseph and the child to Damascus, to the house of a rich man, who protected and provided for them. He nourished many lame and blind persons.

At this time a very valuable article of his was stolen, and no trace of the thief could be found ... (The child Jesus) said – "Such a lame and such a blind man stole the thing." When accused, the blind man said, "How could I see to steal?" and the lame man, "How could I walk to do so?" Jesus said – "The blind man carried the lame man, who then from a shelf took the goods and divided the booty." So the theft was found out. [16]

Muslim legends contain other similar stories about Jesus, all intended to show that he was more than a man, or better, that he was not actually a man. Jesus was, and is, divine. But when people first saw him – walking along the road, sitting on the grass, worshipping in the temple, eating a meal, conversing with his friends – they saw just a natural man. And that is how *we* should first see him.

THE HUMANITY OF JESUS

Too often we look at Christ through the stained-glass windows of two thousand years of tradition and four hundred years of Elizabethan English. Consequently, we see him

---

(16) From an article, *Christ in Mohammedan Literature*; ibid. Vol.2, pages 883, 884.

as a very mystical figure speaking an unreal language, wearing a white gown and a shining halo! [17]

The church has always tended to veer between admiration and dislike of the maleness of Jesus. The early church was repelled by it. Hence they tended to focus so much upon the divine splendour of Christ that he became too much removed from ordinary people. So they turned to Mary instead, interposing her between themselves and Christ. In fact, contrary to popular opinion, the exaltation of Mary to divine status did not begin in the Middle Ages but rather with the dehumanising of Jesus in the 2nd century.

But the Renaissance rediscovered Christ the man, and Western culture once again began to glory in the divine image in men and women (as the ancient Greeks had done during the peak of their culture). Renaissance scholars noticed that even the apostles had chosen to describe our salvation in terms of the Greek ideal (*soteria*), which to them was a quality of perfection both in bodily form, mental wisdom, and in moral conduct (cp. 1 Th 5:23).

The Renaissance brought about a re-discovery of the dignity of the human form, which is nowhere more marvellously revealed than in the Incarnation. Many renowned artists celebrated this divinity within humanity by leaving no one in any doubt that Jesus was a normal boy! Any good illustrated book on Renaissance art will disclose many paintings of a naked and obviously male Infant. This is not a sign of artistic lewdness but of a rediscovery of the sheer wonder of *Emmanuel*, God with us in human form. By contrast, when

---

[17] Barry Chant, in an unpublished text on *Christology*, page 1.

Jesus' cousin, John the Baptist, is included in a painting, he is usually well covered!

However, the Renaissance so humanised Christ that his glory was lost, which a century later the Reformers restored. But they too succeeded too well, for since then the tendency once again has been to focus on the ethereality of Christ and downplay his sweaty humanity. How difficult it is to imagine these ethereal saviours burning with anger, laughing heartily, or ever knowing the bitter-sweet pangs of sexual desire!

If you have an illustrated Bible, or have ever seen a modern painting of Jesus with his disciples, you will know that artists nearly always portray Christ so that he is instantly recognisable – we would probably be offended if they did not do so! Rather, we expect to see Jesus with his garments brighter, his stature more imposing, his hair more golden, his features more handsome, his halo more glowing, and surrounded by a numinous aura. We expect him to be among other people, yet obviously different from them. We could hardly accept an artistic portrayal of Jesus that showed him as a 30-year old carpenter, wearing a sweat shirt and grubby jeans, dusty, dripping perspiration, struggling with primitive tools against the stubborn timber.

The saintly image that most people would prefer may suit their pious urges, but it bears small resemblance to the real Jesus. There is no suggestion in the gospels that Jesus stood apart from other people, or that he was the kind of man who was instantly recognisable in a crowd. On the contrary, it was apparently easy for him to merge with a crowd and to become lost to sight – cp. *Luke 4:30; John 5:13; 8:59; 10:39-40*. Apart from perhaps the Nazareth incident, there is no reason to suppose a miracle on any of these occasions. See also *John 7:1-25*; note the indecision of the people concerning Jesus' identity, whether or not he was the person the rulers wanted to kill.

So we are going to look at Jesus through the eyes of his contemporaries, to see him as the carpenter's son from Nazareth, to see him as he would have appeared to his neighbours, his friends, and his enemies. My intention is to establish his complete humanity. Why is this necessary?

Originally, of course, no one thought to question whether or not Jesus was really a man. If his enemies had supposed him to be anything other than an upstart peasant who could be safely bullied and killed, they would never have dared to lay a finger on him. Even his disciples, before the resurrection, obviously thought of him only in human terms.

It was not until Christians began to ascribe divinity to the risen and ascended Christ that they also began to question whether Jesus of Nazareth had actually been a proper man. Perhaps he had been merely in the guise of a man, like the angel that had appeared to Manoah's wife? (Jg 13:2-3 ff.) This is the great *"mystery of our religion"*, that God was *"manifested in the flesh"* (1 Ti 3:16). The church has ever struggled to grasp this mystery, and to explain it in a way that does no violence to scripture. That means trying to find a way to affirm both that Jesus was truly man, but also truly God.

Jesus himself warned against allowing his humanity to become clouded beneath an over-strong emphasis upon his deity. He made it clear that our perception of his deity will be no clearer than our perception of his humanity. If you lose *Jesus*, you will also lose *Christ*. If you cannot see the *Man of Nazareth*, neither can you see the *Father in Heaven* (Jn 14:8-9; 12:44-45). Discover the man, and you will discover God.

As Martin Luther said – "The deeper we can bring Christ into our humanity, the better it will be for us!"

If we are wise, we will avoid the extremes of the past; we will neither focus too much upon the <u>humanity</u> of Christ, nor upon his *deity*. A true Christian *life* inescapably depends upon a true image of *Christ*. So let us now search for this real man.

Chapter Two

JESUS IN THE GOSPELS

I heard a voice which said, "There is one, even Christ Jesus that can speak to thy condition," and when I heard it, my heart did leap for joy! [18]

HIS ORIGIN

The virgin birth of Jesus will be discussed in a later chapter; but it should be noted here that a better description might be "virgin conception". It was the conception of the baby that was supernatural, not his birth. He was conceived by a miracle; but his actual birth was in every way ordinary, except that he was born in squalid and miserable surroundings, among the dung and stench of a cave that was used to confine animals. [19]

A birth such as this, in such poverty, and into such a humble family, was hardly remarkable. On the contrary, it predisposed many people to insist that Jesus was an

---

[18] George Fox (1624-1691), founder of the Society of Friends, in his Journal 1674.

[19] Justin Martyr (c.150) and Origen (c.200) both claim that Jesus was born in a cave, which Origen says that he had actually seen. The "manger" in which the baby was laid (Lu 2:7) was probably a feeding trough used by animals. That Mary and her baby did not contract any disease from the dirt in which they lay may well be the real miracle which attended his birth (as distinct from his conception).

insignificant and probably illegitimate peasant. It was inconceivable that such a person could be a teacher or prophet in Israel.

His eventual home town, Nazareth, made it even more unlikely that he was destined for greatness (Jn 1:46), and disparaging remarks continued to be made about the seeming doubtful circumstances of his birth (Jn 9:29). The wise men, a few shepherds, and a handful of other people were witnesses of the dazzling star (Mt 2:10) and of the angels' acclamation (Lu 2:13-15); but to most observers the obscurity of Jesus' origins precluded him from being anything more than a humble artisan.

HIS NAME

His real name was "Joshua" [20], a name he shared with thousands of other Jewish boys. "Joshua" was as common in those days as Peter or John are today. As a name it was unremarkable, and by its very familiarity had become undistinguished. There was no indication here that Jesus was anything more than a plain man.

HIS APPEARANCE

I have already suggested that the outward appearance of Jesus was probably ordinary rather than extraordinary. Barry Chant agrees –

---

[20] "Jesus" is the anglicised version of the Greek form of the Hebrew name "Joshua".

His appearance was not unusual. For thirty years he lived in comparative obscurity, [21] accepted as a normal member of society. While he lived among them, his own town folk saw nothing unusual in him. In fact, they were surprised when he started preaching (Mk 6:1-3). Because of his years as a carpenter, his hands would have been rough, his body well-developed and his muscles strong.

He was a good carpenter, too, for his work was well known (Mk 6:1-3). The fact that people were astonished at his authority and learning indicates that he had no specific religious training – that, in fact, he was so obviously a working man, an ordinary man, that to see him as a teacher and miracle-worker seemed strange (Mt 7:28-29, etc.). Further evidence of his normal appearance is shown by the fact that Judas needed to give a sign to identify him (Mt 26:48). [22]

If the bearing of Jesus had been full of majesty and beauty, surpassing that of other men, making him instantly

---

[21] By contrast, think about Alexander the Great, who conquered the civilized world before he was 30 years old, and was found lamenting the fact that there were no more lands for him to rule. See also the *Addendum* on "Child Prodigies". Jesus may have possessed such abilities, but if so, apart from the incident recorded in *Luke 2:41-51*, he gave no indication of them. To his immediate neighbours his talents seemed so ordinary that when he did begin to speak and act as "no other man had ever done," they were first astonished, then frightened, and then angry (4:14-30). (Footnote by KDC.)

[22] Op. cit.

recognisable, his enemies could have found him and arrested him without the help of a betrayer.

Some of the early church fathers agreed with this view. Thus Justin Martyr (c.150), referring to *Isaiah 53:2*, reckoned that Jesus lacked any special physical beauty –

> We have announced him as a child before him, as a root in a dry ground. He hath no form or comeliness, and when we saw him he had no form or beauty; but his form is dishonoured, and fails more than the sons of men.

Then, referring to *Psalm 24:10*, he says –

> For when the rulers of heaven saw him of uncomely and dishonoured appearance, and inglorious, not recognising him, they enquired, "Who is this King of glory?" ... and again ... "When Jesus came to Jordan, he was considered to be the son of Joseph the carpenter; and he appeared without comeliness, as the scripture declared." [23]

Clement of Alexandria (c.200), using the same text, argued that Christ was "unlovely in the flesh;" and Tertullian held to the same opinion, giving the following translation of *Isaiah 53:2* –

> (Christ was) not even in his aspect comely. For "we have announced", says the prophet, "concerning him, (he is) as a little child, as a root in a thirsty land; and there was not in him attractiveness or glory. And we saw him, and he had not attractiveness or grace; but his mien

---

[23] Dialogue With Trypho, chapter 13,36,88.

was unhonoured, deficient in comparison with the sons of men."

However not everyone shared those opinions. Origen (c. 220) allowed that to some people Jesus appeared to have "no form or glory, and his form was without honour, and inferior to that of the sons of men." But he insisted that there were others to whom Christ appeared full of beauty, and he cited David, *"You are the fairest of the sons of men; grace is poured upon your lips"* (Ps 45:2). [24]

He also referred to the Transfiguration (Mt 17:2) as proof that to those who had eyes to see, Christ truly did have "a divine appearance", and an aspect of nobility and glory. So he described

> the changing relation of (Jesus') body, according to the capacity of the spectators ... inasmuch as it appeared to each one of such a nature as it was requisite for him to behold it ... (so that it should) at one time possess a quality, agreeably to which it is said, "He had no form nor beauty," and at another, one so glorious, and majestic, and marvellous, that the spectators of such surpassing loveliness ... should fall on their faces.

> Thus there arose two schools – those who held that Jesus was "fairer than the children of men," among whom were St Augustine, St Ambrose, and St Chrysostom; and those who, in their ascetic reaction against the vices of pagan beauty-worship, declared that he had

---

[24] Against Celsus, 6:75,76,77. For additional comment see the *Addendum*, "On the Appearance of Christ."

"no form nor comeliness" and "no beauty that we should desire him"; among whom we see St Basil and St Cyril of Alexandria. [25]

The fact is, no portrait, nor any reliable description of Christ was produced by anyone who had known him in the flesh. Artists have been obliged to use imagination, with the result that representations of Christ have variously depicted him as unspeakably ugly, a beautiful youth, an idealised and perfect man, a stylised incarnate deity, or an ordinary human being.

THE MARKS OF MANHOOD

So far, in our study of the humanity of Christ, we have examined the witness of the gospels to the fact that he was truly a man. We explored his *origin*, his *name*, and his *appearance*, and found nothing there to belie the reality of his human nature. He was not a deity disguised as a man. Whatever divine nature Christ may possess, his human nature remains intact, genuine and earthy. He was indeed *"in every respect made like we are"* (He 2:14,17).

HIS TEACHING

The teaching of Jesus was different from that of any other at the time. It was forceful and provocative. People were surprised by the authority with which he spoke (Mt 7:28-29; Lu 4:32-36). They were also surprised by the nettling, startling things he said –

> *Learn how to build friendships by using worldly riches (Lu 16:9).*

---

[25] Hastings, op.cit. Volume 1, page 314,315; article, *Christ In Art*.

If your hand entices you to sin, cut it off and throw it away (Mt 18:8).

Everyone who came before me was a thief or a bandit (Jn 10:8).

If you refuse to eat the flesh of the Son of man and to drink his blood, you will never possess any real life (Jn 6:53).

– and several other disturbing sayings could be added to the list.

It is not surprising then, after hearing him say such things, that *"many of his disciples drew back and no longer went about with him"* (verse 66). To them Jesus seemed to be a radical extremist, not at all what they expected from their Messiah!

Another cause of astonishment was his ability in debate. Jesus continually drove his opponents into confusion – not by playing smart, but by the sheer force and perceptive brilliance of his arguments (cp. Lu 20:1-40; Jn 10:34-39).

Nonetheless, he taught, not as a "god" might be expected to do, using amazing prodigies and awesome demonstrations (cp. Mt 4:5-6), but as a man among men, using argument, persuasion, illustration, and the like. He showed the naturalness of his mind by his easy employment of many different forms of speech, such as –

- hard irony (Jn 10:32)

- gentle irony (Mt 6:32; did only the gentiles *"seek all these things,"* or did the Jews seek them even more furiously?)

- blistering sarcasm (Mt 12:27)

- harsh invective (Mt 23:1-36; "woe to you hypocrites! ... you blind guides ... you blind fools ... you whitewashed tombs ... you brood of vipers ... you murderers!")

- satire (Mt 6:3; Lu 16:1-9); and so on.

His bitter denunciations of the religious leaders, his kind words to the poor, provoked the rulers to hatred and delighted the people; but eventually the mob itself turned on him, and they all howled for his blood.

HIS CONVERSATION

Jesus enjoyed social activities, and he displayed an easy familiarity with both men and women. He was an excellent conversationalist, an accomplished raconteur, and all kinds of people wanted him to visit their homes and share a meal with them. One of the most charming (and most profound) stories in the gospel is the account of the wedding at Cana (Jn 2:1-11); but that was only one of many such occasions. Jesus described himself as being quite unlike the ascetic John the Baptist, who *"came neither eating nor drinking."* On the contrary, he *"came eating and drinking,"* and he was a friend even to *"tax collectors"* (Mt 11:18-19).

HIS HUMOUR

Jesus often spoke wittily, and with laughter, [26] a fact that is sometimes obscured by our English versions. Consider the

---

[26] Contrary to those who feel that Jesus never laughed (because he is described as "a man of sorrows"), see (a) those places where Jesus bade his disciples to be merry and glad, even to leap and dance with joy, for reasons that would have been just as compelling for him as for them – Mt 5:11-12; Lu 6:22-23; Jn 14:28; and (b) verses which either state or imply that Jesus did experience exuberant joy – Lu 10:21 (the Greek word = to
– continued on next page

evident humour in the following sayings, selected only from the gospel of *Matthew*. It is hard to believe that Jesus did not speak at least some of these with a chuckle –

> *If anyone smacks you on the right cheek, then let him backhand your left cheek as well (5:39).*
>
> *If anyone compels you to carry a load for one mile, then volunteer to carry it for a second mile (5:41).*
>
> *How can you say to your neighbour, "Let me take the splinter out of your eye," when there is a log in your own eye? (7:4)*
>
> *Do not feed pearls to pigs (7:6).*
>
> *... will be like a crazy man who builds his house in a sandy river bed (7:26).*
>
> *Bait your hook, throw it in the water, open the mouth of the first fish you catch, and you will find a shekel (17:27).*
>
> *A camel may more easily pass through the eye of a needle than a rich man can enter the kingdom of God (19:24).*
>
> *You blind guides, who strain out gnats but then swallow camels ... who scrub the outside of a cup while leaving it filthy inside! (23:23-26)*

---

celebrate, to be exceedingly glad); Lu 15:6,9 (the Greek word = to share joy with others); Lu 15:32 (both Greek words convey the idea of a joyful celebration); Jn 11:15. There are other examples of both (a) and (b) in the gospels.

And let me add this further example from *Mark* –

> *To James and John, Jesus gave the name "Boanerges", that is, "Sons of Thunder" (3:17).*

Could he have done so without at least a smile?

HIS NATURE

There is a divine as well as a human aspect to his nature and personality. He is the Son of God as well as the Son of Man. This divine nature was present in him from the moment of his conception in Mary's womb; it did not come upon him after his birth, it did not merely assume a human covering, say, after he had reached manhood; rather, he was *born* with it. But neither did it impinge upon his genuine humanity and manhood. He called himself a man (Jn 8:40); he was called a man by others (Jn 1:30; 4:29; 5:12; 8:40; 1 Ti 2:5; etc.); and the term *"Son of man"* is used of him some 80 times in the four gospels alone.

His divine nature was submitted to his human form, and had to accept the limitations imposed by a normal range of human faculties and skills. Despite his underlying divine identity, one of the results of the incarnation was that Jesus had to become as we are, and to live as we live. [27] So –

- he had to travel about laboriously (Lu 8:1; Jn 4:4,6).
- he grew hungry (Mt 4:2; Lu 7:34).
- he became weary (Jn 4:6; Lu 8:23).

---

[27] For further comment, see the *Addendum*, "Jesus of Nazareth."

- he had to ask questions and get information (Mk 9:21).
- he had limited knowledge, and, like any man, could know the future only as far as the Holy Spirit permitted him to know it (Mk 13:32).
- he could be indignant when he was treated with discourtesy, and he was pleased when respect was shown toward him (Lu 7:44-47).
- he loved his friends, and formed special friendships (Jn 15:13-15;13:23).
- he loved his mother (19:26-27).
- he understood the urge of patriotism (Mt 23:37-39; Lu 13:34-35).
- he shed tears of disappointment. (Lu 19:41), of sympathy (Jn 11:33), and of bereavement (verses 35-36).
- he experienced the horror of pain (Mt 26:38-39; 27:26; Jn 19:28).
- he burned with moral indignation (Mk 3:5; 10:14).
- he felt the poignant wrench of sudden love (Mk 10:21), and he rejoiced in the warmth of being loved (Mk 26:39).
- he had to steel himself against his friends, and to remain steadfast in fulfilling his vocation (Mt 16:22-23).
- he could be astonished (Mk 6:6), and lonely (Mt 26:37), and angry (Jn 2:15).
- he delighted in children (Mt 19:13-15).

- he delighted in simple things and loved the beauty of nature (Mt 6:26-29).

Finally, he experienced that most human of all sorrows, the one thing inevitable for all men, death (Mt 27:50; Jn 19:34).

Even after death his aspect remained very human. He was shrouded and buried as any dead man would have been. And after the resurrection, despite several extraordinary attributes (such as the power to appear and disappear at will), he was still demonstrably a man in his form and behaviour –

- he was able to walk and talk with human companions (Lu 24:13-35).
- he could still eat and drink, although presumably without necessity (Lu 24:42-43; Jn 21:9-13).
- he was recognisable (Lu 24:31; Jn 20:16).
- he breathed (verse 22); he was substantial; they could feel his flesh and bones; it was Jesus himself, fashioned still as a man (Lu 24:39).

HIS RELIGIOUS EXPERIENCE

The true humanity of Christ is revealed in the nature of his relationship with God, and with Satan –

HIS RELATIONSHIP WITH GOD

Prayer was the foundation of the communion Jesus had with the Father, and he seems to have needed prayer as much as we do – see *Mark 1:35; Luke 3:21*; etc. – except that he never needed to pray the one prayer we need most of all, "Father, forgive me!"

Astonishingly, the gospels make it clear that not one of his close associates was offended by the fact that he never asked for pardon from God. They accepted without protest his claim to be free of sin (Jn 8:46), and apparently admitted that there was something about his fellowship with the Father they had never experienced.

With insight and beauty, H. D. McDonald writes –

> But we must press into the inner court, the holy place of his moral and spiritual life ... of what we may call Jesus' religious relation with God. He certainly knew God in an intimate and personal way. It has been rightly remarked that Jesus was not one of the many seekers after God, not even if we call him one of the successful. He bore witness to God. His understanding of God is a prophetic testimony born out of his inner experience. His knowledge of God was the natural outflow of his intercourse with God. He felt himself to be in possession of God, to be in his presence always ...
>
> Out of this living and felt certainty of God's reality and presence sprang his faith, prayer, joy and obedience with reference to God, and his service and patience with reference to man. His trust in God was real and whole-hearted. He was not nervous and timid amid life's uncertainties, for to him everything was in the Father's hands ...
>
> Jesus belonged to God first, then to man, in that proper order. It is for this reason that he sought that place of solitude before his times of service. He waits that he may be alone. He knows he needs God, though he shares his life.

He is sure of God all the day through, and all the way along; but he must talk to him, he must get together with God.

Has he not taught us that man needs no spectators, no congregation, no priests when he prays? (Mt 6:6). Thus he prays (Mk 1:35). His praying is no parade; it meant something. He prayed because he had need to pray; that he might find refuge under the shadow of the Almighty wings; that he might renew his innermost being in the strength of God; that he might find, in his reverent trust in his Father, nerve for the ordeals of living ...

It was in this attitude of faith, prayer and joy he rendered his full obedience to the will of God. Thus was the religious relation to God at once both natural and spiritual; the same that is required of all men, but which none but he has met. [28]

HIS RELATIONSHIP WITH SATAN

Christ, we are told, "suffered" under the blows of temptation. His relationship with the devil was one of conflict. He too had to combat satanic wiles and deceit. You can be sure that Jesus did experience real temptation, as Satan tried to provoke in him the lust of the eyes, the lust of the flesh, and the pride of life (1 Jn 2:16; Lu 4:1-13). He was *"tempted as we are in every possible way, yet he did not sin"* (He 4:15). But because he himself knew the bitter suffering of temptation (2:18), he is now able to *"empathise with us in*

---

[28] <u>Living Doctrines of the New Testament</u>, Pickering and Inglis Ltd., London; 1971; page 28,29.

our weaknesses" (4:15), and *"to help those who are tempted"* (2:18).

It is doubtful if any other human being has been so savagely attacked by temptation as Jesus was – *"He prayed with such agonising fervour that sweat was wrung from his brow and fell to the ground like great drops of blood"* (Lu 22:44).

Such intensity of temptation strongly shows how totally Jesus shared our human condition. He must have been a true man, or the temptations would not have been genuine – *"God cannot be tempted by evil"* (Ja 1:13) – but a man can.

HIS MIRACLES

The wider significance of the miracles done by Jesus will be dealt with in more detail in other places, but in this chapter we do need to see how his contemporaries reacted to them. The extraordinary works of Christ affected people in different ways –

There were some people for whom even a small demonstration of the power of God was sufficient to prove the divinity of Christ. Thus only one instance of supernatural insight was enough to make Nathanael exclaim, *"Rabbi, you are the Son of God! You are the King of Israel!"* Even Jesus was surprised by this easily won response; so he answered, *"You say that you believe? Yet I said only that 'I saw you under the fig tree!' I tell you, you will see much greater things than that!"* (Jn 2:45-50)

Some of the other disciples were harder to convince; but they too eventually allowed that Jesus' miracles showed him to be *"the Christ, the Son of the living God"* (Mt 16:13-17).

But his miracles did not lead to universal recognition of his divinity. Some said he was demon possessed (Mt 12:24); others called him a man of God (Jn 10:20-21); others acknowledged him as at least a great man (Mt 8:27). No one was really sure (Mt 16:14).

SUMMARY

How then did Jesus appear to his contemporaries, the people among whom he lived prior to his death? It is evident they saw him as a man, although a strange man. No one doubted that he was human – it would never have occurred to them to think him anything else; but what kind of man, they found hard to explain.

Christians believe that there is only one explanation of this dilemma – *to assert that while Jesus was truly human, he was also truly divine.* Most of the rest of this book, along with *Volume Two*, will demonstrate the deity of Christ. But we are not yet quite ready to advance into heavenly territory. There is still a little more to say about the man, Jesus of Nazareth.

What the *gospels* show us about the true humanity of Christ, is confirmed by the NT *letters*. This witness is especially effective, for it comes from writers who by then were fully convinced that Jesus should be called *"Wonderful Counsellor, Mighty God, Everlasting Father, Prince of Peace"* (Is 9:6). Yet while the NT letters certainly are full of references to the present glory, dominion, and exaltation of Christ, they also contain many statements like the following –

- In every way he had to become just like his brothers and sisters (He 2:17).

- He was born looking like an ordinary male, and he took upon himself a true human nature (Ph 2:7-8).

- Jesus of Nazareth was a man whom God himself attested among you (Ac 2:22).

- As by a man came death, so also by a man has come the resurrection of the dead (1 Co 15:21) – a passage in which Adam and Jesus are linked together, for both of them were "men".

- There is one mediator between God and men, the man Christ Jesus (1 Ti 2:5).

- He was born of a woman, born under the law (Ga 4:4).

And to those witnesses we could also add the later reflections of two gospel authors – of *John* (1:14) who declared that *"the Word became flesh"* (that is, assumed a human nature); and of *Luke* (3:23-28), who carefully traced the lineage of Jesus right back to Adam – a fruitless exercise, if Luke had not believed that Jesus and Adam were of the same human form and substance.

Chapter Three

WHAT HIS MANHOOD MEANS

Why was it necessary for the Messiah to appear in human form? Why did he not appear as a marvellous divine emanation? Why could he not have stepped onto the earth in the glory of his deity? That issue is raised in several places in the NT, and various answers are given. Here are some of them

HIS HUMANITY SANCTIFIES OUR HUMANITY

By the will of God we have been sanctified through the offering of the body of Jesus Christ once for all. (He 10:10, KJV)

The willingness of Jesus to dwell in the human body the Father prepared for him (verse 5), has brought a magnificent sanctity to our human frame. How often in the past this craving, thirsting, weak and wearisome flesh has mocked all our pretensions to dignity; how often it has jeered at our spirits as they strove to discover beauty in our human condition. But no longer. The Son became *"Emmanuel" – "God Among Us."* He condescended to take on human form, to be made just as we are made, to live as we must live, to be as we must be; thus our humanity has now been coloured with a hue of ineffable glory.

This awesome transformation has been captured by Henry Hubert Hutto, in his poem *Imago Dei* – [29]

> Not quite furry, not quite bald,
> The ablest and most awkward of the primates,
> Always is something or other inordinately –
> Bare on a beach, obscene; robed, absurd,
> As on his hind legs neighing
> Of his dignity.
> (His rochets and rockets, thrones and symphonies,
> Wall-to-wall carpeting, power steering,
> Virtues, touchdowns, sexual attainments.)
> Queens have caries,
> Boxers, musclebound, grow weak.
> Prelates defecate and even prelates
> Are undignified on toilet seats.
> Sculptors are not made of marble
> And they too have warts.
> The saints sin, and have bellybuttons.
>
> The ablest and most awkward of the primates,
> Not quite furry, not quite bald,
> Faces wars and want and looking-glasses,
> Making systems, singing, building, carving, striving,
> Moon-going, loving –
> Is flayed for goodness, unresisting,
> Looks on circles and sees alternately
> Zero and Eternity,
> And says another, an immanent Breath,
> Includes his own.

---

[29] Copyright *Christianity Today*, 1976. Used by permission.

Once I looked upon my body as an ingesting, sweating, defecating, malodorous, decaying obscenity. I thought it a foul jailor, a savage iconoclast, a defacer of all in me that might have been glorious and divine. It seemed that highest nobility and flesh could never dwell together. But Christ exposed all those fancies as lies. My body, in all its parts and functions, has been made holy by him. He will not permit me to despise it. It is now the lovely temple of the Holy Spirit, the agent by which I glorify God (1 Co 6:10-20).

So Jesus, by the fulness and vitality of his own manhood, teaches us to guard against that false piety which wants to destroy our humanity. He surely has scant patience with those who say that truly religious people must struggle to eradicate, or at least subdue, all that is warmly human in them – who forbid a saint to laugh, or weep, or to enjoy the pleasures of food, art, music, literature, sport, human society, and the like – who say that man is born only to preach and pray – that only those who are hermits or ascetics, either in practice or in spirit, can be truly holy.

Christ would not have denied that there is a place in the larger kingdom of God for those who, by disposition or by the call of God, are led into a hermit's cave, or to an ascetic austerity. But he would have insisted also that there is room in the kingdom for those who dwell in a king's palace, who sit on high thrones, who wield great power, and possess vast affluence. Nor is there room lacking for ordinary people living ordinary lives, compounded of labour and laughter, joys and sorrows, pain and pleasure, and all that belongs to pursuing happiness and fulfilment in life.

Christ showed favour to princes as well as paupers, to humble men as well as the great; and he looked with kindness on that multitude of ordinary people who also have their part in the economy of God. Hence there was room in the church equally for the wealthy courtier Manaen, the tentmaker Saul, the black Symeon, the compassionate Jew Barnabus, and the Hellenistic Jew Lucius (Ac 13:1).

There was something about the manner of Jesus that enabled all kinds of people to commune with him comfortably. No one felt uneasy in his presence merely because there was a difference in lifestyle, culture, dress, learning, or social standing.

There was nothing about Jesus to suggest that only those who, like him, were born Jews, and who dressed and behaved in a Jewish manner, could become his close friends. He was all things to all men (cp. 1 Co 9:19-23). He gave a sanctity to many different conditions and styles; he approved all that is not specifically forbidden to this person or that.

Because of Jesus, I can rejoice that I am a man and not an angel, a human being and not a spirit, possessing a body and not incorporeal, and that *"in my flesh I shall see God"*! (Jb 19:26)

THERE IS REDEMPTIVE SIGNIFICANCE IN HIS HUMANITY

> *Jesus said to them, "I am the bread of life; those who come to me will never hunger, and those who believe in me will never thirst ... and the bread that I am giving to bring life to the world is my body ... With all my heart I tell you, unless you eat the flesh of the Son of Man and drink his blood, you will never possess any real life. But those who eat my flesh and drink my blood already have eternal life, and I will raise them up at the last day." (Jn 6:35, 51-58)*

If Christ had not come in the flesh there would be no redemption for fallen man. Jesus was emphatic – the nourishment our souls needed to escape death and to live for ever could come only through his body and blood – that is, through what his humanity alone was capable of creating for us.

We are an amalgam of body and spirit. He is no man who has body alone, but not a spirit; nor spirit alone, but not a body. If we are to be redeemed, then this redemption must embrace both body and spirit. Hence Christ was *"put to death in the body, and made alive in the spirit"* (1 Pe 3:18), thus providing a basis upon which God may now *"sanctify you wholly, and keep your entire spirit, soul, and body blameless"* in preparation for the rapture of the saints (1 Th 5:23-24).

Christ died a *double* death – *physically* (Mk 15:37); and *spiritually* (verse 34)[30] – so that we who were already doubly dead might escape bondage and be born into the endless and indestructible life of heaven (cp. Ro 8:9-11). [31]

---

[30] This "spiritual death" must, of course be understood metaphorically. Christ could not literally die spiritually, any more than we can. "Death" in relation to the spirit means separation from God. Furthermore, it could only have been the man Jesus of Nazareth who was briefly cut off from the Father when "he became sin for us" The eternal Logos could never for a moment be divided from the Father.

[31] Isaiah also describes this double death and double redemption – physical (53:9); and spiritual (vs. 6, 10a). There is a mysterious significance in verse 9, which reads literally – "they made his grave with a rich man in his deaths (plural)." Perhaps there is a suggestion here that this was no simple death, but a complex one – as if he had in a sense died over and over again, making atonement for sin and creating healing for his people.

THIS MAN IN HEAVEN GUARANTEES OUR ENTRANCE

The hope set before us in Christ is a strong and firm anchor of the soul, a hope that presses into the very throne-room of God ... where Jesus has gone as a forerunner on our behalf. (He 6:19-20)

Across the centuries the great question was asked – "Even if sin should be pardoned, and righteousness ascribed to the trusting servants of God, how can we be sure that it is possible for a human being, either in time or eternity, to enter the blazing presence of God?"

Scripture itself raised the issue – *"Who among us can survive the devouring flames? Who among us can endure the eternal fire?" And does it not say, 'No human can see the face of God and live'? And, 'God is surrounded by impenetrable light. No one has ever seen him, nor ever can see him.'"* (Is 33:14; Ex 33:20; 1 Ti 6:16)

What proof is there that I, a mortal man, will ever be able to stand without fear before the glorious throne of God, or that I may ever participate in that same glory, and not be obliterated by it?

The apostle gives an answer in one word *prodromos* = "forerunner". The Man Jesus has already entered the Holy of Holies in heaven, to remain unharmed in the very Presence of God. Humanity is already seated at the right hand of the Majesty on High (He 1:3). A Precursor has gone before us; a precedent has been established. There can no longer be any doubt. Those who are properly identified as friends of the Forerunner not only have free access to God now, through prayer, but their footsteps will one day echo, as his have already, in the sacred throne room, which at this moment only he and the chiefest angels dare enter. But he *is* there, now, in Adam's form; the guarantee that any other child of Adam who chooses to join him may safely do so.

In Bible days, *prodromos* was used in battle to describe an advance guard of soldiers, who were given the task of clearing the way for the following army. In naval warfare it was used to describe the ship, perhaps the most powerful vessel in the fleet, which was given the honour of leading the other ships into battle – as, for example, in Nelson's day, great ships-of-the-line took an advance position, and received the brunt of the enemy's fire-power when two fleets clashed.

That point is sometimes missed by commentators who liken the "forerunner" either to the high priest in ancient Israel, or to a runner in an athletic contest. But the high priest entered the holy of holies only once a year, and only as the representative of the people, none of whom dared to follow him. And in an athletic contest, the winner of the race is running for himself, not for the other contestants.

But the idea of *prodromos* is not that of one man entering, or winning, to the exclusion of all others; but rather, the idea of a *pioneer*, of one who is blazing a trail for others to follow; or, of one who is establishing a *precedent*, which others may then freely copy; or, of an *advance party* whose task is to clear the way for the main force; and so on. It is the idea expressed by the old Jewish sage (using the same Greek word) – *"You sent wasps as forerunners of your army, to destroy the enemy little by little"* (Wis 12:8); and see also, *"I will send hornets before you, and they will compel the Hivites, Canaanites, and Hittites to flee from you in panic."* (Ex 23:28,).

Jesus himself expressed the idea exactly –

> *I am going to prepare a place for you, and I will come again to take you back with me, so that where I am you may be also. (Jn 14:3)*

Jesus has marched in triumph across the territory through which we must march, and toward the same kingdom. He has splendidly cleared the way for us to follow; for without his pioneering we could never have traversed that land.

Let your soul then be steadfast, anchored to this sure hope – the Man who is now in heaven has established for ever a pathway into the holiest, upon which you may walk with joy, to come where he is, to sit where he sits, and to inherit with him the kingdom of the Father. [32]

HE IS ABLE TO SYMPATHISE AND HELP

> *He had to be made just like his brothers and sisters, so that he might become a sympathetic and faithful high priest ... And now, since he himself has been tempted, and suffered, he is able to help us when we are tempted (He 2:17-18).*

> *We have a high priest who is able to sympathise with our frailties. That is because in every way he himself was tempted just as we are, although he did not sin. Remember that whenever people choose a high priest from among themselves, they appoint him to act on their behalf before God ... And because he himself is beset with human weakness he can deal kindly with those who are ignorant and even with the wayward ... So let us boldly draw near to the throne of mercy, so that we may receive pardon, and find grace to help whenever we are in need (He 4:15-5:2).*

---

[32] Is 35:8-10; Mt 19:28; 25:34; Re 3:21

In the hour of judgment, no condemned person will be able to accuse God of tyranny, nor argue that, because God has never felt the bitter force of temptation, his judgments are therefore unjust.

We have a legal principle that an accused person must be tried by his peers. Nearly 800 years ago, *Magna Carta* established this rule –

> No freeman shall be taken, or imprisoned, or outlawed, or exiled, or in any way harmed, nor will we go upon him, nor will we send upon him, *except by the legal judgment of his peers or by the law of the land (Clause 39*, italics mine*)*.

It is inherent in our sense of justice to believe that only those who have felt the temptations suffered by an accused person are fit to determine whether he is innocent or guilty. In our law courts an accused person is allowed to challenge anyone whom he deems unfit to be a member of the jury that is to try him.

Likewise in the day of final judgment, every person will be judged by him who is pre-eminently the Peer of all men, Jesus. He is our peer, and our fit judge, because he has fully shared our human condition, and he has endured the thrusting persistence, the onslaughts, of all manner of temptation.

He made himself the Peer of every man when he suffered the temptations that beset –

- the scholar (Lu 2:46-48)
- the general (Mt 26:53)
- the poor (Mt 8:20)
- the popular (Mt 21:9)
- the rich (Mt 4:8-9)
- the forsaken (Mt 26:56; 27:46)

- the betrayed (Mt 26:48-51)
- the hungry (Lu 4:2-3)
- the lonely (Mt 26:40)
- the powerful (Lu 9:54-55)
- the orator (Lu 4:22)
- the afflicted (Lu 9:22)
- the wise (Lu 20:39-40)
- the despised (Jn 8:48; 9:29)
- the simple (Mt 11:29).

And to that list many others could be added.

Together, they mean that no one will be able to stand before the throne of Christ and accuse him of being removed from their pain, of not having walked where they walked, of not being tempted as they were tempted. He was made like us "in every respect"; he suffered under the same merciless pressure of temptation; yet without sin. There is none so right as he to be the judge of the whole family, of which he is himself a full member.

Jesus himself cited his human experience as the basis upon which the Father had qualified him to be the judge of all humankind – *"The Father has given the Son authority to exercise judgment, because he is the Son of Man"* (Jn 5:27).

But he became a man, not just to qualify himself as our Judge, but much rather to qualify himself as our Friend. Among men it sometimes happens that those who successfully resist temptation lack sympathy for those who fall. They become harsh and unfeeling in their condemnation of weaker men. But not so this great high priest of ours. Although sin found no place in him, and he remained utterly pure in mind and body, no self-righteousness has made him proud, nor is he swift to censure those who are not so strong as he. The tears he shed have made him kind toward those who weep – *"He deals kindly with the ignorant and wayward."*

For this reason, we who are tempted may with unswerving confidence draw near to the throne of grace, knowing that the tempted Christ will be merciful to our weakness, and that the triumphant Christ will be strong to help us in our weakness (He 2:18; 4:16; 7:25).

BECAUSE HE LIVES, WE TOO SHALL LIVE

Jesus for a short time was made lower than the angels. But now, because he willingly suffered death, he is crowned with glory and honour. Indeed, it was by the grace of God that he tasted death on behalf of everyone ... He did this because he wanted to be like us, to share fully in our nature, even to the point of embracing death. Also, his plan was, through death, to destroy him who had power over death, that is, the devil (He 2:9,14).

Because we are flesh and blood, and therefore subject to death (verse) 15), Jesus also, if he would be our Deliverer, had to share the same nature.

There is special emphasis here on the extraordinary mystery of the incarnation of Christ. Because it seems so unbelievable that he who is now crowned with glory and honour, and who sits at God's right hand (1:3), had walked as a man among other men, the apostle stresses Christ's true humanity again and again. There can be no doubt about it. He was indeed flesh and blood, just as we are, and he died just as we die. Death was as real and as terrible for him as it is for us. The grave fastened its grip upon him. But it could not hold him.

He lifted himself bodily from the grave on the third day (Lu 24:39-40).

Now forever the question is answered affirmatively – *"If a man dies, can he live again?"* Yes! There is a Man in heaven. He died. He lives. He has taken our human form into the very presence of the Eternal God. He sits upon the throne of God. Even the highest angels prostrate themselves in delighted adoration at the feet of that Man. And now he is the guarantee that all who die in him will themselves conquer death and become co-heirs with him of the kingdom of God (Ro 8:18-23, 16-17).

Chapter Four

CHRIST — THE ETERNAL LOGOS

There is a legend that St Augustine (early 5th cent.), while he was struggling to comprehend the Trinity, met the Christ-child on the sea-shore. Augustine failed to recognise the boy, and watched with amusement as he toiled to scoop out the ocean with a sea shell. The great bishop tried to show the young Jesus the futility of using such a meagre tool for such a mammoth task. But the boy sharply replied, "My use of a shell to tame the rolling waves is much less foolish than your belief that your mind is large enough to comprehend the Trinity!"

It is indeed absurd for any finite mind to pretend to encompass the infinite Deity. But this does not mean that our efforts are vain, only that, in the end, both _theism_ and _atheism_ rest upon an act of faith. In the end, neither theist nor atheist can prove the truth of what they affirm. To say "there is no God" requires just as much faith as to say "there is a God". Neither proposition, if one is looking for some kind of mathematical, scientific, or objective proof, can be established beyond doubt. Thus scripture itself says —

> **Faith** *is the substance of things hoped for, the evidence of things not seen* (He 11:1).

> *By* **faith** *we know that the entire universe was created by the word of God, so that what is seen was made from things that are invisible* (He 11:3).

> *Without **faith** it is impossible to please him, for anyone who comes to God must believe that he is, and that he is the Rewarder of those who diligently seek him* (He 11:6).

Note too that a proven Christ no longer requires any act of faith. God could easily demonstrate his reality (as many have begged him to do — cp. Is 64:1-2), [33] but then, where would any space be left for freely offered love and service?

But to say that *absolute* proof is lacking does not mean that there is *no* proof. On the contrary there is much evidence [34] to support all the major propositions that Christians make concerning Christ and the gospel.

CHRIST – PRE-EXISTENT WITH THE FATHER

Toward the end of the first century an unwanted infant boy was left on the roadside by his parents. He was picked up by a person who made a living out of collecting and selling abandoned children. In Rome the boy was sold to a wealthy matron, Rhoda, who eventually freed him. He soon displayed remarkable business acumen and began to amass a fortune. He also married and had several children, and he and his family began to attend church. But then a time of persecution fell upon the church. His wife and children

---

[33] The prophet longed for a visible demonstration of Yahweh's might. He wanted God to open the heavens and come down upon the land in a blaze of glory and majesty. But ordinarily that is just what the Lord does not do. Mostly, he prefers the "still, small voice" (1 Kg 19:12).

[34] For a substantial presentation of the arguments in favour of belief in God, see my book Strong Reasons.

recanted and denounced Hermas, who was arrested and imprisoned. There he became aware of many personal faults, deeply repented, and resolved that if he were freed again he would devote his life, not to getting rich, but to the service of Christ. Upon his release he set about regaining the love and respect of his wife, who herself repented and returned to the faith. His children, it seems, remained rebellious against the gospel, but Hermas stayed true to his vow and was content to serve the church in Rome as a deacon for the remainder of his life.

Somewhere around the year 130, Hermas began to compose an allegory, *The Shepherd*, which, in a series of visions, similitudes, and other devices, presents a body of teaching about Christ and the church. For several centuries it was enormously influential and Hermas himself was named one of the Fathers of the Church. In many parts of the early church his book was treated and quoted as scripture. It was finally dropped from the canon in the fifth century, but it is still in print today, usually titled *The Shepherd of Hermas*.

It contains the first known reference to an ancient piece of theology known as **_adoptionism_**.

 (1) Has Jesus always existed as the Son of God with the Father, or did he have no existence prior to his birth in Bethlehem nearly 2000 years ago? *Adoptionism* argued that Christ was an ordinary man who, because of his extraordinary virtue and amazing works, was *"adopted"* – that is, elevated to deity by an act of the Father. [35]

---

[35] The technical term "apotheosised" (noun, apotheosis) comes from a Greek word meaning "to make someone a god, to deify a person".

This was an easy view for the ancients to accept, because of the many contemporary myths about humans who had been apotheosised. [36]

(2) The doctrine eventually assumed the following outline –

- Jesus was born of a virgin by an act of the Holy Spirit
- after his virtue had been proved through 30 years of testing, the Holy Spirit fell upon him, and he became the Christ
- but he was not yet divine, until by his resurrection the Father transformed him into the Son of God (Ro 1:4; and cp. Ac 2:32-33).

The purpose of the doctrine was to explain the mystery of how Jesus could be both God and Man, and how he could suffer and die if he is divine. It failed because scripture plainly shows the doctrine of Christ's ***pre-existence.***

The pre-existence of Christ is demonstrated in many places –

- Jesus knew that he had come from God (Jn 13:3).
- I know where I came from . . . I came from God (Jn 8:14,42; and cp. 12:27; 18:37).
- The glory I had with you before the world began (Jn 17:5).
- Christ is the Lord from heaven (1 Co 15:47).
- Although Christ was rich, yet for our sake he became poor (2 Co 8:9).

---

[36] See the myths about Hercules, Odysseus, Asclepius, etc; and note also the deification of many Roman emperors, beginning with Julius Caesar, then Augustus.

- God sent forth his Son (Ga 4:4).
- Although he had the very nature of God, Christ emptied himself, and appeared among us as a man (Ph 2:6-8).
- All things in heaven and on earth were created by Christ (Cl 1:15-16).
- Before Christ ascended into heaven, he first descended onto the earth (Ep 4:8,9).
- God sent his one and only Son into the world (Jn 6; 1 Jn 4:9-10).

The **biblical** proposition is that through Christ, humanity has now been added to deity; but **adoptionism** turns scripture around and says that deity was added to humanity. But that would exalt man above God, for only the *lesser* can be added to the *greater*! We therefore cannot doubt that Christ, as the eternal Logos, existed with the Father for ever before he was incarnated for 33 years as Jesus of Nazareth; and that now, since his ascension, he continues for ever enthroned at *"the right hand of the Majesty on high"* (He 1:3). [37]

CHRIST – FORETOLD IN THE SCRIPTURES

AMAZING PROPHECIES

I have heard it said that there are more than 300 predictions in the OT that were fulfilled in Jesus of Nazareth. Whether

---

[37] How the Logos could remain eternal in heaven while the Man was on earth is discussed in Emmanuel – Part Two.

that is so or not, Jesus himself did tell us to *"search the scriptures"* (Jn 5:39).

Peter Stoner lists 8 of those prophecies (Ps 22:16; Is 53:7; Mi 5:2; Zc 9:9; 11:12,13; 13:6; Ma 3:1). [38] He then provides a set of calculations to show that the chance of any one man (from the time the OT was completed) fulfilling all 8 prophecies in his own life is 1 in 10^{17}. Here is some idea of what that means – cover the whole of NSW [39] with 20c coins to a depth of one metre; throw into the pile one marked coin; stir up the heap; ask a blind man to find the marked coin! The odds against him succeeding are 10 to the 17th power [40] (that is, the number 10 with 16 zeroes added to it).

Add another 8 prophecies, and the odds increase to 1 in 10^{45}, which would equal enough 20c coins to cover a circle with an area 30 times greater than the distance from the earth to the sun – that is, more than 4 thousand million kilometres.

If you increase the number of prophecies to 48, the odds then become an astonishing 1 in 10^{157}, which exceeds the number of grains of dust in our entire universe of perhaps 100 thousand million galaxies!

We are still only talking about less than 50 oracles. Yet, from a list I once compiled myself, I know that there are at least

---

[38] Science Speaks, by P. W. Stoner & R. C. Newman; Moody Press, Chicago; 1976; ch. 3, "The Christ of Prophecy". The calculations in the next two paragraphs are also based on Professor Stoner's illustrations.

[39] The State of New South Wales (NSW) in Australia has an area of approximately 800,000 sq km (310,000 sq mi), which equals about 10% of the Australian mainland.

[40] That is, the number 10 with sixteen zeroes added to it. Ten to the second power (10^2) is 100; ten to the third power is 1000, etc.

100 oracles in the *Old Testament* that relate to Christ, and some scholars would double or triple that number. In any case, fulfilled Bible prophecy represents a staggering improbability brought into reality. But consider the peril! Suppose one or more of those oracles had failed? The credibility of the entire Book would be darkened, and doubt cast over every one of its doctrines. To give to the world a Book containing so many prophecies that might easily have failed is to take an enormous risk. It demonstrates breathtaking boldness.

Contrast this boldness on the part of scripture with (say) the *Koran*, which rejects any need for predictions of future events, save those oracles that deal with the coming resurrection and judgment. [41]

Further, many of the biblical oracles describe detailed specifics, leaving no doubt of the actual event when those details were fulfilled. Thus —

- Daniel's prophecy of the 70 weeks (Daniel 9) places the arrival of the Messiah at the time of Jesus Christ (see the *Addendum*, "The Seventy Weeks.")
- Jesus was to be born in Bethlehem (Mi 5:2), *of a virgin*. (Is 7:14), and then
  - to live in Nazareth of Galilee (Is 9:1-2);
  - to minister and preach to the poor and the needy (Is 61:1-2);
  - to preach to the Gentiles (Is 42:1);
  - to be rejected by the rulers (Ps 118:22);

---

[41] See the *Addendum*, "The Koran," for some examples.

- to be betrayed by a friend for 30 pieces of silver (Zc 11:12-13);
- to be pierced. (Zc 12:10); and
- to suffer the piercing of his hands and feet (Ps 22:16) – which was written several centuries before crucifixion was invented by the Romans.

- See how detailed Jesus himself found the prophecies to be – *Luke 18:31-33; 24:27,44-47; etc.*

Such an amazing succession of wonderfully fulfilled oracles, against almost incalculable odds, should give us more than enough reason to maintain unwavering confidence in all the promises of God. Bible prophecy, as the apostle said, does indeed *"shine like a radiant light in a dark place"* (2 Pe 1:19-21).

WHY THEN DID THE JEWS REJECT HIM?

Some, of course, did accept Christ (Lu 2:25-28, 36-38). Others were blind, perhaps because –

- they were confused by the mixture of first and second advent oracles that exists in the OT and they could find no reliable way to separate them.
- they wanted a political revolution, not a moral reformation.
- they wanted a Jewish Empire, not a Gentile Church.
- they wanted to confirm the establishment, not to destroy it.
- the prophecies could be understood only by revelation (Lu 24:45).

But nothing anyone could do could hinder –

THE GREAT PLAN OF GOD

When the time had fully come, God sent forth his Son (Ga 4:4).

"WHEN THE TIME HAD FULLY COME"

Why did Jesus not come earlier? Because the time was not yet ripe. But only forty years before Jesus was born, Julius Caesar was murdered on the floor of the Roman Senate. Civil war broke out and Caesar's adopted son Octavian, though only in his early twenties, seized the hour. Through a series of brilliant campaigns he made himself the first emperor of the Romans, ruled a vast empire, and gained the honorific Augustus. The scene was then finally set, as it had never been before, for the appearance of the Messiah. The world was now ready for the gospel – [42]

Spiritually – Paganism was dying. The myth-based religions of Greece and Rome were already 1000 years old, while in Egypt the goddess Isis had been worshipped for at least 2000 years. Those ancient faiths had in a measure brought satisfaction to many generations, but now the world had dramatically changed, and everywhere a new spiritual hunger had sprung into existence. [43] Although the Jews had built synagogues in every city (Ac 15:21) and their monotheism was appealing, it remained too exclusive for most people; so there remained a world-wide hunger for a better way to God.

---

[42] The next few paragraphs occur in a slightly different form in my book <u>The World's Greatest Story</u>.

[43] See also the *Addendum* – "Isis and Osiris".

Culturally – In the early 4th century BC, Alexander the Great created what was then the greatest empire the world had seen. He achieved his extraordinary goal of spreading Greek language, art, literature, and culture throughout the known civilised world. Greek became the *lingua franca* of the Greek and Roman world, a vehicle of communication that could be understood everywhere. [44]

Greek, too, was the first language ever to exist that was capable of handling abstract ideas. It is no accident that philosophy as we understand it developed in ancient Greece. No Egyptian nor Babylonian, nor any Hebrew prophet, could ever have produced the ideas (say) of Aristotle – their languages simply did not allow such thoughts. They had no words to express metaphysical ideals. Thus a Hebrew prophet like Isaiah could speak about "justice" in concrete terms of *doing* justly; but "justice" as an eternal principle, as an entity separate from human action, would have been for him an inaccessible concept.

So, there is no actual theological thought in the *Old Testament*; nor, without Greek, would there have been much of it in the *New Testament*. Paul's magnificent letters to the *Ephesians* and *Colossians*, with their lofty notions, their

---

[44] After the collapse of Alexander's empire, the Greek culture he had carried to every part of his dominions remained, and "became the chain for the spread of Christianity. Without this common language of Greek, Christianity could never have spread beyond Judaea." (<u>Alexander the Great</u>, by Robin Lane Fox; The Folio Society, London, 1997; pg. 487.) By the 2nd century A.D. the barbarian invasions of the Roman Empire had begun and the use of the Greek language in the West began to collapse. The Latin and Greek worlds became divided, but the window of opportunity had been open long enough for the gospel to be spread throughout the Mediterranean world and beyond to the British Isles. The church was well-established and could no longer be eradicated.

spiritual perceptions of righteousness, truth, holiness, justification, and the like, had to await the creation of a language that could give voice to them.

Politically – The patterns of Roman government and law provided an example that made the forensic ideas of the gospel (with its message of justification by faith) everywhere comprehensible. [45] The genius of the Greeks was in art, literature, and philosophy; the genius of the Jews was in religion; but the genius of the Romans lay in law and administration.

A hundred years or so before Paul, when Roman hegemony had not yet been established, nor its concept of the rule of law widely understood, the letters to the *Galatians* and the *Romans* would have been meaningless. Prior to Rome, the law was whatever the monarch said it was, and could be changed in a moment by some royal whim. But (at least in theory) by the time of Paul it was understood everywhere that no one, not even the emperor, stood above the law. Thus it became easy to do what before would have seemed absurd to most people, that is, to transpose the idea of the rule of law to heaven, and to recognise that even the Lord God is subject to the law's demand for justice, truth, and integrity.

Practically – The Roman roads and Roman fleet made travel safe for everyone. [46] Plutarch tells a story about

---

[45] For example, a hundred years earlier Paul could not have written in Romans 7:1 the words – *"Certainly you will understand what I am about to say, my brothers, because all of you know about law!"* (GNB) Note also the idea of the rule of law in Acts 25:16.

[46] By contrast, note Sirach's brave comment, only two centuries earlier (34:10-12) – "Those who have little experience will have little knowledge. But someone who is much travelled will be full of common sense. When I travelled, I saw many things, so that now I

– continued on next page

Julius Caesar that shows the beginnings of the eventual successful Roman purge of piracy from the Mediterranean –

> Caesar put to sea and made for Bithynia. After a short stay there with Nicomedes, the king, in his passage back he was taken near the island of Pharmacusa by some of the pirates, who, at that time, with large fleets of ships and innumerable smaller vessels, infested the seas everywhere.
>
> When these men at first demanded of him twenty talents for his ransom, he laughed at them for not understanding the value of their prisoner, and voluntarily engaged to give them fifty. He presently despatched those about him to several places to raise the money, till at last he was left among a set of the most bloodthirsty people in the world, the Cilicians, only with one friend and two attendants. Yet he made so little of them, that when he had a mind to sleep, he would send to them, and order them to make no noise. For thirty-eight days, with all the freedom in the world, he amused himself with joining in their exercises and games, as if they had not been his keepers, but his guards. He wrote verses and speeches, and made them his auditors, and those who did not admire them, he called to their faces illiterate and barbarous, and would often, in raillery, threaten to hang them. They were

---

understand more than I can put into words. Indeed, I was often in danger of death; yet I escaped unharmed, thanks to all the things I have learned by experience."

greatly taken with this, and attributed his free talking to a kind of simplicity and boyish playfulness. As soon as his ransom was come from Miletus, he paid it, and was discharged, and proceeded at once to man some ships at the port of Miletus, and went in pursuit of the pirates, whom he surprised with their ships still stationed at the island, and took most of them. Their money he made his prize, and the men he secured in prison at Pergamus, and he made application to Junius, who was then governor of Asia, to whose office it belonged, as praetor, to determine their punishment. Junius, having his eye upon the money, for the sum was considerable, said he would think at his leisure what to do with the prisoners, upon which Caesar took his leave of him, and went off to Pergamus, where he ordered the pirates to be brought forth and crucified; the punishment he had often threatened them with whilst he was in their hands, and they little dreamt he was in earnest. [47]

Thus, by the time of Paul, piracy at sea was no longer a serious threat, and apart from natural perils he could take ship with a reasonable certainty of reaching his destination.

Socially – With Augustus, there began an era of 300 years of comparative peace unparalleled in the ancient world. [48]

---

[47] <u>Lives of the Noble Grecians and Romans</u>, "Caesar"; John Dryden translation.

[48] The "Pax Romana" brought to an end centuries of endless warfare. The citizens of the empire were so grateful for its benefits, that they readily called Caesar the "Saviour" of the world (which is
– continued on next page

This world-wide peace, the *Pax Romana*, along with the protection afforded by the Roman authorities, and the laissez-faire structure of Roman society, were among the main reasons why the apostles were able to travel freely, and to carry the gospel to the ends of the empire and beyond. [49]

Prophetically – as in the above notes.

So in the days of Augustus Caesar the time was indeed *"fully ripe"* for the appearing of the promised Messiah, and therefore

"GOD SENT FORTH HIS SON"

- To reveal God – John 6:38. Christ showed that <u>all</u> could freely address God as Father.
- To save the lost – Luke 19:10. This is a picture unique in sacred literature, of *God* seeking man; for in all other religions the picture has been, and is, that of man seeking after God (with the consequence that their gods become made in a human image, instead of the reverse).
- To ransom the slaves – Matthew 20:28
- To destroy the works of Satan – 1 John 3:8
- To build his church – Matthew 16:18
- To be crowned king – John 18:37.

---

perhaps one reason why the term is seldom used in the New Testament). See also the *Addendum*, "The Emperor as Saviour."

[49] The occasional bursts of imperial persecution of the church did not significantly alter this situation. (During the first 300 years there were 54 emperors, of which only 12 actively persecuted the church; and of them only a couple made any serious attempt to destroy the entire church.)

Chapter Five

THE LORD FROM HEAVEN

After the day of Pentecost the church began to spread far beyond the borders of Palestine. Thousands of people joined it who had never met Jesus in the flesh. Their first encounter was not with the Man from Nazareth, but with the Lord from Heaven, the glorious Son of God. As these Christians became more deeply convinced of the deity of Christ it seemed ever more improbable, even impossible, that he had ever been an ordinary man.

Some people began to whisper that Jesus' human nature had not been real, that he had not been truly human.

Eventually John was compelled to warn the churches that anyone who denied Jesus had come in the flesh belonged, not to Christ, but to antichrist! (1 Jn 4:1-3).

That change of focus is fascinating. The wonder of Christ for the first disciples lay in the fact that the Jesus they had known in the flesh was now glorified; but for later Christians, the wonder of Christ lay in the fact that their heavenly Lord had once endured humiliation among men, and then death.

H. D. McDonald finely expresses this contrast –

> For the original disciples the astonishing thing was that Jesus, whom they knew and whose companions they were, and who had been put to death as a common criminal, should now be exalted to the throne of God. To Paul, the very reverse was the astonishing thing. He had been confronted by the living Christ on the Damascus road and his immediate reaction

was to acknowledge him as Lord. The One who had so overwhelmed him by the sheer grace of God was declared to be the exalted Jesus. He was seen by Paul's new inner sight to have a place in the realm of divine lordship.

For Paul the glory of Christ lay in the humiliation which brought him to within the human sphere to accomplish his divine work of salvation. For the other disciples the wonder lay in his exaltation from the human sphere, having died a death which was revealed to be on account of man's sin.

Peter saw the glory of Christ against the background of his lowly ministry. His thought travelled from the Christ of the Galilean road to the Lord of the excellent glory. Paul's took the reverse direction – for him the amazing thing was that the Lord of the eternal throne should meet him on the Damascus road. [50]

We are able to traverse both realms. Before you began to read these pages, you probably knew Jesus overwhelmingly as the glorified Lord. But then you walked with me into Judea, and we became intimately acquainted with the man of Galilee. We visited his home in Nazareth, we welcomed his firm handshake, we shared a meal with him, and lively conversation. But now he is gone, and if we would see him again we must look upward, and discover him reigning in supernal splendour from heaven's highest throne. Behold! he is the *Prince of Peace*, the *Wonderful Counsellor*, the *Everlasting Father*, the *Mighty God*! (Is 9:6)

---

[50] Op.cit., page 146.

How can this be? Surely such a transformation is unbelievable? If he really is the *Mighty God*, how could he ever have become a man? If he were really a man, how can he now be called the *Everlasting Father*?

Some of the answers to these questions lie in the mystery of the incarnation, which we shall examine later. In this present chapter I want to concentrate on the fact of Jesus' deity, just as in previous chapters I concentrated on the fact of his humanity. I will not try to explain here how humanity and deity can dwell together in one person, but simply try to prove that Jesus possesses a divine nature as fully as he possesses a human nature. I did not always believe that. Indeed, for some years I thought that Jesus was much less than God, and that it was blasphemous to give him equal honour with the Father. Many hymns were banished from my repertoire, such as –

> Holy, holy, holy, Lord God Almighty! ...
> God in Three Persons, blessed Trinity!
> – Reginald Heber

> For the beauty of the earth,
> For the beauty of the skies, ...
> Christ, our God, to thee we raise
> This our sacrifice of praise.
> – F. S. Pierpoint

Such sentiments were anathema to me! And in fact from the days of the apostles there have been groups of people who have refused to accept the deity of Christ. Let me outline some of their arguments, and then tell you what made me change my mind –

OPPOSING ARGUMENTS

Some of the common arguments against the deity of Christ are –

- The scriptures emphatically declare that God is one, not three – *"Hear, O Israel, the Lord our God is one Lord"* (De 6:4; and see also Is 45:5; 46:9; Mk 12:29).

Unlike the Father, who has neither beginning nor end, there was a time when Jesus did not exist – he was *"the beginning of the creation of God"* (Re 3:14); he is *"the first born"* of the Father (He 1:6); he was *"begotten"* by God (Jn 1:14).

> *If the Father begat the Son, he that was begotten had a beginning of existence; hence it is clear that there was a time when the Son was not. (Arius, c. 300 A.D.)*

- Jesus asserted that the Father was greater than he – "The Father is greater than I" (Jn 14:28). "I can do nothing on my own authority ... I seek not my own will but the will of him who sent me" (5:30) ... "This is eternal life, that they know thee, the only true God, and Jesus Christ whom thou has sent" (17:3) ... "The living Father sent me, and I live because of the Father" (6:57; RSV).
- Other scriptures portray Christ as less than the Father in person and in office, and as being separate from the Father –
- No one has ever seen God except his only Son. He is dearest to the Father's heart, and he has made God known *(Jn 1:18)*.
- There is one God, the Father from whom everything came, and for whom we all exist. And there is one Lord Jesus Christ, through whom everything came, and because of whom we all exist *(1 Co 8:6)*.
- When everything is subjected to God, then the Son himself will also be subjected to God who has put everything under his authority *(Mk 15:28)*.

- Jesus is expressly described as a Man, in contrast with God – "Jesus of Nazareth was a man whom God attested among you by mighty signs, wonders and miracles, which God did by him in your sight" (Ac 2:22) ... "There is one God, and there is one mediator between God and man, the man Christ Jesus" (1 Ti 2:5).
- Key texts used by trinitarians are either
- <u>mistranslated</u> (e.g. Jn 1:1 should read, "In the beginning was the Word, and the Word was with God, and the Word was a god"); or are
- <u>spurious</u> (e.g. 1 Jn 5:7, *"There are three that bear record in heaven ... "* is missing from the best Greek manuscripts).
- The idea of a Trinity is illogical, impossible to comprehend, nowhere clearly taught in scripture, a source of endless controversies, and pagan in origin. Concerning its illogicality, issues like the following can be raised –
- if Jesus is truly God, then who ran the universe during the three days he lay in the tomb?
- how could he forsake himself at Calvary (Mk 15:34)?
- when he prayed (Jn 11:41), was he addressing his prayers to himself; and so on?

Many years ago such arguments persuaded me to deny the deity of Christ. I thought of him as being more than an angel, but less than God. He possessed *divinity*, but not *deity*. He was mighty, but not Almighty. He was a god, but not God. Then one day I was reading the *Gospel of John*, and I came upon a strange verse that I had never before noticed.

It changed my thinking about Jesus.

John tells about the time when Jesus, weary of the obduracy of the people, *"departed and hid himself from them"* (12:36). He had done *"many miracles in front of them, yet they refused to believe in him"* (verse 37). Then John adds this comment – *"(These things happened) so that the oracles spoken by the prophet Isaiah would be fulfilled ... 'He has blinded their eyes and hardened their heart'"* (38-40). Then John makes this remarkable declaration – *"Isaiah said this because he saw Jesus' glory and spoke of him"* (verse 41).

Those last words arrested my attention. When did Isaiah see the glory of Christ? When did Isaiah describe that glory? I could remember Isaiah's prophetic description of Christ as *"the suffering Servant"* of God (53:1-12); but I could not recall any place where the prophet had seen Christ in glory. So I looked again at what John had written.

He says that Isaiah saw the glory of Christ on a certain occasion, which the prophet described in the words, *"God has blinded their eyes and hardened their hearts"* (Jn 12:40-41).

What was that occasion? It is found in *Isaiah 6:1-10*, with the passage quoted by John being found in *verses 9-10*. But the chapter actually begins thus –

> *In the year that King Uzziah died I saw the Lord (Adonai) sitting upon a throne, high and lifted up; and his train filled the temple. Above him stood the seraphim ... and one called to another and said – "Holy, holy, holy is the Lord (Yahweh)* [51] *of Hosts; the whole earth is*

---

[51] "Yahweh" is now universally accepted as a more correct rendering of the ancient Hebrew name of God than the mediaeval form, "Jehovah".

> *full of his glory"* ... *And I said, "Woe is me ... for my eyes have seen the King, the Lord (Yahweh) of Hosts!"'* (RSV, slightly modified)

Isaiah says that he saw the King, who is Yahweh, the great God of all heaven and earth, and the One of whom it is said, *"Hear, O Israel, the Lord (Yahweh) our God is one Lord (Yahweh)"* (De 6:4).

But John says that the King seen by the prophet in that stunning vision was none other than Jesus! The glory that filled the temple was the glory of Christ; **_he_** was the mighty God acclaimed by the seraphim as they hid their faces from his transcendent majesty!

The conclusion is inescapable – <u>*Yahweh*</u> in the Old Testament, and <u>*Jesus*</u> in the New Testament, are the same.

So I began again to search through all the scriptures, and to discover more of the glory of this Christ who had been veiled from my sight.

PROOFS OF THE DEITY OF CHRIST

It is often said that the doctrine of the deity of Christ depends more upon pagan speculation than it does on scripture; or that Greek philosophers, not the apostles, gave birth to the doctrine of the Trinity.

Those claims are false. While there are some references (such as those mentioned above) which at first sight suggest that Christ is less than God, there are many others that clearly state or imply his full deity. When the *whole* testimony of the NT is taken into account, an overwhelming impression is left of the equality the Son shares with the Father.

Again, it is true that the apostles nowhere attempt to formalise their concepts of the Godhead, and the word

"Trinity" (⁵²) is not used in scripture; yet the information contained in the NT made those later doctrinal developments inevitable.

Two things, in fact, have compelled the Church to affirm the full deity of Christ –

- the witness of the NT, which on almost every page ascribes to Christ titles, attributes, and works that are rightfully the properties of deity alone.
- the collective experience of Christian people, who, in their worship of Christ, their prayers to him, their relationship with him, irresistibly behave toward him as though he were God.

It is certain that the apostles were driven by this common experience of Christ to exalt him higher and higher in their thought. Perhaps they began by seeing him only as a man, then as a prophet, then as a unique Son of God, but within a very brief period after his resurrection they had begun to speak of him in terms that previously they would have used only of God.

---

(52) The earliest known use of "Trinity" occurs in a 2nd-cent work, Theophilus to Autolycus – "For the sun is a type of God, and the moon of man. And as the sun far surpasses the moon in power and glory, so far does God surpass man. And as the sun remains ever full, never becoming less, so does God always abide perfect, being full of all power, and understanding, and wisdom, and immortality, and all good. But the moon wanes monthly, and in a manner dies, being a type of man; then it is born again, and is crescent, for a pattern of the future resurrection. In like manner also the three days which were before the luminaries, are types of the Trinity, of God, and His Word, and His wisdom." (Bk. II, Ch. 15; emphasis mine) Theophilus was the 6th bishop of Antioch. The quotation comes from a screed he wrote circa 180 to a pagan friend, hoping to convert him to Christianity.

Immediately after his ascension, they began to worship him, to address prayers to him, and to work miracles in his name. They soon realised that he was everywhere, and that they could be separated from neither his presence nor his power.

This rapid ascription of divine qualities to Christ, by people who had been trained in the discipline of a strict monotheism, was quite astonishing. It could only have arisen out of the direct testimony of the Holy Spirit, and out of the undeniable force of their personal experience of Christ.

Across the centuries there have been numerous attempts to reduce the glory of Christ. In our present community the main exponents of a limited Christ are the *Unitarians*, the *Jehovah's Witnesses*, and the *Christadelphians*, along with some other clusters of sectarians and genuine Christians, including one or two Pentecostal groups.. But neither in the past nor the present have the teachings of such groups gained approval by the major part of the church.

The vast majority of Christians, even if they cannot refute the doctrinal arguments of the Arians [53], still deeply understand that their salvation is dependent upon a dynamic personal relationship with Christ – in other words, they must walk with him, worship him, adore him, talk to him, as though he were indeed God. *But that is idolatry if he is not God!*

So then, let us confirm this Christian instinct, firstly from the claims of Jesus himself, and then from the witness of the NT as a whole.

---

[53] Arius (early 4th century) was an early proponent of a form of unitarianism. His life and teachings will be more fully discussed in a later chapter.

CHRIST WAS AWARE OF HIS DEITY

Belief in the deity of Jesus is based pre–eminently upon his own claims. It is important to realise this, because it is sometimes said that the gospel Jesus himself preached was simple, uncluttered, free from metaphysical mysteries, until the apostles (notably Paul) added a mass of complicated dogma to it and muddied its pure water.

That is nonsense.

There are no mysteries in the NT letters that are not raised first in the gospels. In fact, the mysteries and complexities inherent in the words and actions of Christ surpass anything found in the remainder of scripture. It is impossible to read the four gospels intelligently and not be profoundly disturbed, even angered, by things that are written there.

After searching continuously through the gospels for some six decades I am still dismayed, lacerated, infuriated, awed, inspired, humbled, or filled with wonder at what I find. I am hardly any closer to a full understanding of them now than when I first began. But I am sure of this – in those four books the deity of Christ is more clearly drawn than anywhere else in scripture.

In the next chapter we will look at Jesus' self-awareness as a boy, and as a man, and then at the claims he made concerning himself.

Chapter Six

THE MAN WHO IS GOD

In ancient Greece there was a group of priestesses of Apollo who were known as the Sibyls. They were organised into nine orders, based upon the geographic location of each oracle. To those nine the Romans added a tenth, *The Tibertine Sibyl,* which gained its name from the ancient Etruscan town of Tibur (modern Tivoli). Lactantius [54] describes the nine Greek Sibyls, and then says of the Roman extra that she was "worshipped at Tibur as a goddess, near the banks of the river Anio, in the depths of which her statue is said to have been found, holding in her hand a book. The senate transferred her oracles into the Capitol." [55]

The Sibyls, according to Lactantius, insisted upon belief in one supreme God, and produced a number of oracles that later Christians interpreted as referring to Christ and the coming Day of Judgment.

The most famous of the Tiburtine oracles, according to legend, was spoken to Augustus Caesar, during whose reign Jesus was born (Lu 2:1). Augustus was troubled by the clamour of some members of the Senate, who wanted to acclaim him as a god. Seeking wisdom (unknowingly on the very day of the Nativity), at midnight he went down to the

---

[54] Early church historian circa 240-320.

[55] *The Divine Institutes*, Bk. One, Ch. 6; The Ante-Nicene Fathers, Vol. Seven; pg. 16. The transfer of the oracles to the Capitol was, of course, a mark of high honour, and shows the respect that was given to them.

Tiburtine shrine on the banks of the Tiber. He asked the oracle if there were a greater ruler than he already living, or was there one yet to come? The Sibyl showed him first a vision of the sun surrounded by a golden circle. Then he saw, in the midst of the circle, a lovely young woman reclining and suckling a baby. The Sibyl declared that this child, now born, would become the greatest ruler of all time, and a voice echoed from above saying, "This is the altar of Heaven!" *(Ara Coeli)*

Augustus at once humbled himself, bowed in worship, and later built on Capitol hill a monument to commemorate the divine revelation. He also interpreted the vision as meaning that he should reject the pleas of the Senate to deify him, and he insisted that they must be content to honour him merely as a man. [56]

In the seventh century a church, *Santa Maria Ara Coeli*, [57] was built on the site, which still exists in Rome, and claims to house in a side chapel the very altar built by Augustus.

The legend, of course, is dubious, but there is no doubt that Jesus was indeed born during the reign of Caesar Augustus, revered by wise men, adored by shepherds, acclaimed by angels, and surrounded by the aura of the Star of Bethlehem. But what did he think about himself?

---

[56] He was, however, after his death on August 19th, A.D. 14, deified by the Senate on September 19th. That is, the Senate decreed that he should be included among the official state gods and thus become a member of the Roman pantheon.

[57] "The Church of Saint Mary of the Heavenly Altar."

THE SELF-AWARENESS OF CHRIST

AS A BOY

When did Jesus first become aware of his true identity?

That is a difficult question. If his humanity was real, then he plainly had to grow in understanding, as any human infant must do. We must reject, for example, the Muslim fables mentioned in our first chapter, in which the baby Jesus was supposed to have spoken like an adult. He did not speak while he was nursing at his mother's breast, he gurgled. And when he was a toddler, he prattled, as all normal toddlers do.

Scripture leaves us in no doubt that Jesus, just as we all must, had to grow in his knowledge of himself and of the world around him – *Luke 1:80; 2:40, 52.*

Nevertheless, by the time he was twelve years of age he had developed an awareness of God that was surprising for one so young (Lu 2:41-50). Thus he was in the temple, *"listening to the doctors of the law and asking them questions"* (vs. 46).

Presumably he was seeking to understand the scriptures better, and from the scriptures to understand his own identity and the purpose of his life. Perhaps he was beginning to realise that he was the one of whom the prophets had spoken, but if so, this understanding must still have been rudimentary.

But although he did not yet fully comprehend his own identity, it is clear that Jesus, at twelve years of age, had developed an intense awareness of God. He was already enjoying intimate fellowship with God as his Father. The unusual character of this fellowship is shown by his use of the personal pronoun – "my Father," rather than "the Father." So, when his mother said to him, *"Your father and I have been anxiously searching for you,"* he replied, *"Did you not realise that I would be in my Father's house?"*

It is unlikely that Jesus was intending to rebuke or correct Mary by this reply, and even less that he was being deliberately rude. His use of the expression *"my Father"* was simply an unconscious response to the idea aroused by her words, *"your father."* This response shows how real God had already become to him. The strength of his personal commitment to his heavenly Father was so great that it transcended all other loves or loyalties. His supreme motive, the one controlling impulse in his life, had already become obedience to the will of God.

How unusual, even mystifying, this level of spiritual awareness was in a 12-year old boy is shown by Luke's comment, *"They were not able to understand what he meant by those strange words"* (verse 50). [58]

It seems evident, therefore, that out of his growing knowledge of God and of scripture, there arose in Jesus an increasing realisation of his own identity, of his real origin, and of his mission. In this too he set us an example – for it is part of the gospel to affirm that no one can truly discover

---

[58] Part of Mary's astonishment may have arisen also from the fact that devout Jews in those days did not speak about "My Father". Rather, Yahweh was thought of as the Father of the nation or of the tribe, but not of the individual. The idea was akin to the old British way of describing their monarch as "Sire", thus maintaining a conceit that he was the progenitor and protector of his people. So Jesus may well have been the first Jew ever to think of Yahweh as "Father" in an intimate and personal sense. Yet, surprisingly, God himself had long ago expressed a yearning that his people would indeed so address him (Je 3:19). But (prior to the coming of Jesus) they had continually failed to perceive the Lord's meaning, nor could they ever summon enough boldness to cry, "My Father!"

himself until he first discovers God, and that the will of God is revealed in scripture. *That is how it is with us; and that is how it was with Jesus.*

So Jesus, learning more deeply each day that God was in a peculiar sense his Father, came to realise the uniqueness of his Sonship, and then to realise that he must be the One of whom all the prophets had spoken.

But that realisation probably did not become fully established in his mind until he was well into his adult years, and perhaps not until the moment after his baptism, when the Father spoke to him from heaven (Mt 3:17).

AS A MAN

There can be no doubt, though, that by the time Jesus had reached full manhood he was completely aware of his real identity and of his mission. That is shown beyond any doubt by the extraordinary things that happened when he was baptised by John in the river Jordan (Jesus was about 30 years old). The Holy Spirit descended on him, in the shape of a dove, and the Father spoke from heaven – *"You are my beloved Son; with you I am well pleased"* (Lu 3:21-22).

At that moment, the Father publicly acknowledged Jesus as his special Son, declared his sinlessness, and anointed him to be the Messiah of Israel. All of which would have been meaningless if Jesus had not, either prior to or in that moment, understood who he was. That he did understand is shown by his prayer for the Holy Spirit to fall upon him, after he had been baptised by John, and by the fact that he did not demur at the honour John paid him (Lu 3:21; Mt 3:14; Jn 1:29-34).

From that time on the sayings of Jesus reveal a staggering contrast between the most exalted self-assertion and the most humble self-effacement. As Charles D'Arcy has said, qualities which in any other person would be quite incompatible, somehow combine inoffensively in Jesus – "all seems natural and inevitable in the portrait as we find it in the gospels." [59]

How is this so?

Simply, it is because the gospel portrait of Jesus is not fiction, but a natural description of Jesus' own deep and true awareness of his actual identity. He could not say or do any other –

> *If I said, I don't know God, I would make myself a liar like you; but I do know him, and I keep his word* (Jn 8:55).

The perfect humility of Christ revealed the gracious character of the Father; but it is in his self-assertion that Christ revealed his claim of equality with the Father. To give all the instances of that self-assertion would require a reprint of much of the gospel story, for hardly a page lacks an expression of Jesus' astonishing sense of his divinity. But here are some of the most striking examples –

- he declared his pre-existence with the Father (Jn 6:62; 8:14,15; 13:3; 17:5).
- he gave to his personal disciples a status equal to that of the prophets who were the servants of Yahweh, thus making himself equal with God (Mt 5:11-12).
- he demanded absolute obedience from his disciples, and a personal commitment that should properly be given only to God (Mt 16:24-28).

---

[59] In Hastings, op.cit., Vol.1, pg. 363.

- the devotion he required was to be given not just to his words, nor to the kingdom, but to Jesus himself (Mt 10:37-39).
- he insisted that the eternal destiny of every human being depended finally upon each person's attitude to himself (Mt 10:32-33).
- he made a clear distinction between himself and all other messengers of God – they were merely *"servants"*, but he is *"the beloved Son"* (Lu 20:13).
- he claimed that the Father would not act independently of his presence and approval (Mt 18:19-20; Jn 14:13; 15:16; 16:26-27).
- he proclaimed himself the great Judge who would preside on the Day of Judgment; but to the OT prophets, this Judge could only be Yahweh, which means that Jesus equated himself with the God of Israel (Mt 25:31-46; and cp. Ps 96:13; 98:9; Jl 3:11-12; etc.).
- he claimed also that judgment would be made on the basis of the relationship the nations had sustained to himself and to his disciples (Mt 25:34,40,45).
- he claimed a special relationship with God, shown by his continual use of the expression, *"my Father"* (not *"the Father,"* or *"your Father,"* or even *"our Father"* (Mt 18:35; and many other places).
- he astounded the people by the personal authority he claimed for his teaching, even above that of Moses and the divinely given law (Mt 7:28-29; 5:20,22,26,28, 32,34,39,44; etc.).
- he called himself by inference the Son of God in *Matthew 21:15-17*.

- he made the startling assertion – *"Everyone who came before I did was a thief or a robber!"* (Jn 10:8) Commentators are much embarrassed by that stark saying. The dozen or so that I consulted all insist upon restricting it in one way or another. They apply it to spurious messiahs, false prophets, and the like. Those explanations may be true. But it seems to me equally probable that Jesus meant precisely what he said – that is, when measured against his own divine perfection, all other priests, prophets, sages, teachers, rabbis *were and are inexorable robbers of truth and thieves of the glory of God*. So am I. Why? Because the finest, the sweetest, the most pure of my writings are inescapably overshadowed by the mortality and corruptibility of a fallen man. At best I am like a man looking through a piece of smoky glass (1 Co 13:12); at worst I am all but blind. And so were and are all except Jesus.

Notice that Jesus did not say, *"The Lord says to you ... ,"* as, for example, the other disciples would have said; nor did he use the first person pronoun in the way the prophets did, speaking as the mouthpiece of God (cp. Ho 6:4-6; and many other places). When Jesus said, "I say to you," he meant just that, "*I* say to you." He was claiming a personal authority equal to that of Yahweh in the OT, who spoke through the prophets. As D'Arcy comments –

> In such passages our Lord declares himself greater than Abraham, David, Solomon; greater than the Temple, the Sabbath, the Law; he claims for himself all the homage and devotion of which the hearts of men are capable; he calls himself "the King" and describes himself as the Judge of all nations; he demands as his right that honour which

belongs to God alone. Yet he is among men as "he that serveth". (Lu 22:37) [60]

(And apart from the references already quoted, see also Jn 8:58; Mt 22:45; Lu 11:31; Mt 12:6; Mk 2:28.)

But perhaps the most astonishing passage is this –

> *My Father has put everything into my hands, and he is the only one who truly knows the Son; and no one knows the Father except the Son and those to whom the Son chooses to reveal him. If you are worn out and overburdened come to me, and I will give you rest. Pick up the yoke I give you, put it on your shoulders, then let me teach you. I am gentle and gracious, and you will find in me a deep inner rest. My yoke is easy to carry. My burden is light to bear (Mt 11:27-29).*

There Christ makes six great affirmations about himself and his work – [61]

- his limitless power and authority – for *"all things"* are in his hand.
- the greatness and mystery of his Person – for he can be *"known only by the Father"*.
- the uniqueness of his relationship with the Father – for he alone truly *"knows the Father."*
- all other people are restricted in their knowledge of the Father – for they can know the Father only so much as the Son *"chooses to reveal him"*.

---

[60] Ibid. pg. 472.
[61] Suggested by a summary in D'Arcy's article, Hastings op. cit.

- he is himself the source of human satisfaction, healing and salvation – for if they come to him they will find *"deep inner rest"*.
- in him there is no conceit, but only truth, with that patience and condescension that is finally possible only to the Almighty, who has no fear that his kindness can be turned against him – for he said, *"I am gentle and gracious."*

In all this, however, it is strange that Jesus did not claim in so many words to be the Messiah, nor to be equal with God. Rather, he preferred his hearers to draw their own conclusions about him (cp. Jn 5:18; Mt 16:16-17). And the instinct of his most devoted disciples, from the beginning until now, has been to accord him the highest possible glory, to give him an honour equal to that given to the Father.

Nothing less will satisfy the self-awareness underlying the words of Jesus himself.

Nothing less will satisfy the demands made upon true believers by their personal experience of Christ. Our perception of the Saviour is identical to his perception of himself – he not only *"called God his Father, but made himself equal with God."*

Chapter Seven

THE POWER OF GOD

No one could make claims about Jesus surpassing those he made about himself. The following list is not exhaustive, but it does include most of the more startling things Jesus professed. Try to imagine a man, or a preacher, coming up to you today, and asserting such things about himself!

If the claimant should happen to look like a god, or even an angel, it might not be difficult to believe him. But when his appearance is that of just an ordinary man you would feel bound to pronounce him insane – unless of course he happened to be Jesus!

There was something about Jesus that convinced people (except for his enemies) that he was neither mad nor bad, but simply speaking the truth.

HIS CLAIM OF POWER OVER DEATH

Jesus asserted his personal authority over death, which in Israel was reckoned to be the sole prerogative of God (Jn 2:19; 10:18; and cp. Ps 68:20; 118:17,18; De 32:39; 1 Sa 2:6.)

Knowing he had power to raise himself from the dead, Jesus was able to claim the same power over all the dead. It is difficult to see anything less than an assertion of deity in these incredible words –

> *What I am telling you is absolutely certain – the hour is coming, and indeed has already arrived, when the dead will hear the voice of the Son of God. Those who believe what he says will live. This is because the Father is the*

> *source of all life, and he has made the Son also to be the source of life ... So do not be amazed by what I say. The hour is surely coming when all the dead will hear the voice of the Son and will come out of their graves ... For just as the Father raises the dead and restores them to life, so also the Son gives life to whomever he pleases (Jn 5:25-29,21).*

What Jesus claimed was later confirmed. He did raise himself from the dead, and by his resurrection established for ever his universal dominion. Hence Paul could write about

> *the good news about God's Son, who was descended from David in respect to his human identity, but was declared with great power to be the Son of God by his resurrection from the dead. He is Jesus Christ our Lord (Ro 1:3-4).*

And John, in his vision saw Christ triumphant, fell at his feet in terror, and then heard him proclaim from heaven –

> *Don't be frightened! I am the first and the last, and the one who lives for ever. I died, but look! I am now eternally alive, and I hold the keys of death and of hades (Re 1:17-18).*

HIS CLAIM OF AUTHORITY AS A TEACHER

The teaching of Jesus was unique, original, and filled with authority. The Rabbis spoke (as we do) *from* authority; but Jesus spoke *with* authority. The prophets said, *"Thus saith the Lord;"* but Jesus said, *"I say ... "* (Mk 1:22; Mt 5:21).

Whence came that authority? It could only have come from his personal awareness that there simply was no greater authority than his own. He did not teach by argument, nor by debate, nor by logical persuasion; but by plain declaration. He commanded!

More importantly, thousands of good people instantly felt the rightness of his command. They accepted without question his authority. They knew that this Man, who spoke like no other man had ever spoken, did not do so with delegated authority (like that of a prophet,) but with an authority inherent in his own person.

A. Martin writes –

> Jesus taught neither as the scribes (Mt 7:29), nor as a prophet (Mt 11:9). And this because of his own nature and the nature of his message. He came not as (an ordinary) teacher (would come), compelling assent by the complete answer to every difficulty, silencing disputes with arguments. He was more personal and spiritual. His teaching did not profess to offer an absolute intellectual proof of itself which must convince all sufficiently intelligent persons. It claimed the belief of all men, but not on the ground of its incontrovertible evidence; on the ground, rather, that all men were created to be good, and to know the truth, and would know it if their perceptions were not dulled and distorted by sin. It convinced only by a process which at the same time purified. He made his message not an argument, but a force. [62]

Yet who has this kind of right and authority except God?

---

[62]   Op. cit.

He Claimed Freedom From Sin

Jesus was the only good man who has ever lived who was not a seeker after God. He did not have to seek God, for he was already in a state of perfect union with God (Jn 10:38; 17:7,11,21-23). He came, not to find God, but to bear witness of God, whom he knew perfectly, and by whom he was perfectly known. But such knowledge of God is not possible to one whom the corruption of sin has seized, for sin darkens the mind (cp. Jn 3:19; 4:17-18; Ro 3:10; etc.).

Jesus, however, was able to claim unbroken communion with the Father because he was also able to claim complete holiness – there was no sin in him of any sort. Mark these sayings –

> *I weigh up every matter, and my conclusions are just, because I am not seeking to impose my own will but rather to fulfil the will of the Father who sent me ... Which of you can prove me guilty of sin? ... I will no longer be able to spend much time with you, because the ruler of this world is coming. He has no power over me. But I will do just as the Father has told me, so that the world may know that I love the Father (Jn 5:30; 8:46; 14:30).*

Even demons were compelled to acknowledge his holiness! (Mk 1:24; Lu 4:34).

Now in this respect, Jesus stands apart from all other saints in history. One of the chief marks of sainthood has always been a deep awareness of sin. The more closely the saint has approached God, the more intensely aware he or she has become of the sin that stains every human soul.

When Isaiah saw God, he cried in despair, *"Woe is me! For I am lost! I am a man whose lips are unclean ... yet my eyes have seen the King, the Lord of hosts."* (6:5).

Paul could not do otherwise than describe himself as *"the foremost of sinners,"* and cry, *"O wretched man that I am!"* (1 Ti 1:15; Ro 7:24).

The godly bishop of Hippo, whose soul was enraptured with the love of Christ, was still constrained to write –

> Who am I? What am I like? Of what evil am I not capable, in either deed or word or will? But you are good and merciful Lord ... If I didn't have that hope I would be desperate. But I believe that in Christ you will heal all my weaknesses, and they are many and great, many and great; but your medicine is even greater ... You know my weakness and my ignorance ... As a beggar, I yearn to be filled by him in the midst of those who eat and are satisfied. [63]

Consider also the man whom history records as living more continuously in the presence of God than any other human being, except Jesus, and perhaps Enoch. It was said of him, by a reverend superior –

> that his principal aim during more than forty years "in religion" has been to be always with God and neither do, say, nor think anything which might displease him ... He has now made such a habit of this practice that he receives divine assistance at all times and places; and for about thirty years his soul has been excited

---

[63] Augustine of Hippo (354-430); translated by Sherwood E. Wirt, <u>The Confessions of Augustine;</u> pg. 119,127,128; Lion Publishing, Tring, Herts, U.K.; 1971. In the original, the excerpts can be found in IX (1) and X (43).

by interior joys, so continuous and so overpowering that, to prevent them being manifest outwardly, he has had to take refuge in behaviour that savours more of silliness than of sanctity.

Who was this man? We know him as Brother Lawrence. And about himself he wrote –

> I look upon myself as a leper, full of corruptions, and the most wretched of men who has done all sorts of wickedness against his king. Seized by remorse, I confess all my evil deeds to him, I implore his pardon. I cast myself into his hands that he may do what he wills with me ... The more I pray to be acceptable to his heart, the more weak and despicable I seem to myself ... It is thus that I look upon myself from time to time in his holy presence. [64]

Even the austere and unworldly Thomas à Kempis warned his readers –

> Therefore acknowledge thyself to be unworthy of heavenly consolation, and deserving of much tribulation ... A good man findeth abundant cause for sorrow and tears; for whether he considereth his own condition or that of his neighbour, he perceiveth that none can escape tribulation. And the more strictly a man weigheth himself, the more cause he findeth for

---

[64] Brother Lawrence (1611-1691), <u>The Practice of the Presence of God</u>; tr. by Donald Attwater; pg. 55,74,76; Burns and Oates, London; 1977.

sorrow. Our sins and vices are truly causes for sorrow and inward compunction; yet so enwrapt are we in evil that we are seldom able to apply ourselves to heavenly things.

And, enjoining a "mean estimation of oneself in the eyes of God", he confessed –

> I will speak unto my Lord, though I am but dust and ashes. If I esteem myself to be anything more, lo, Thou dost confront me, and my sins bear true witness against me, the which I cannot refute. But if I abase myself, acknowledging my nothingness, and rid myself of all self-esteem, reducing myself to the dust I am, Thou wilt confer Thy grace upon me, Thy light will be nigh unto my heart, and all self-esteem, be it ever so little, will be swallowed up in the valley of my own nothingness, and shall perish for ever. There Thou showest me myself, what I am, what I have been, and what I have become; for I am naught, and I knew it not. If I be left to myself, lo! I am nothing, and utterly infirm; but if thou suddenly lookest upon me, I am forthwith made strong again. and filled with new joy. How great and marvellous a thing it is that I am so suddenly lifted up, and so benignly embraced by Thee; I, who, of mine own weight, constantly sink downward to the lowest depths. [65]

The saintly Edward Taylor (c.1644-1729) lamented –

---

[65] Thomas à Kempis (1379-1471), The Imitation of Christ; tr. by George F. Maine; pg. 65,129; William Collins Sons & Co. Ltd., London; 1977 reprint.

> My case is bad. Lord be my advocate. My sin is red – I'm under God's arrest.

> – and by that confession he simply reflected the cry of all those before him and since who have striven to achieve a holy life.

Or consider the tortured soul of St Simeon Stylites as described by Alfred Tennyson in his dramatic eponymous poem – [66]

> Although I be the basest of mankind,
> From scalp to sole one slough and crust of sin,
> Unfit for earth, unfit for heaven, scarce meet
> For troops of devils, mad with blasphemy,
> I will not cease to grasp the hope I hold
> Of saintdom ...
> O Lord, thou knowest what a man I am;
> A sinful man, conceived and born in sin ...
> Good people, you do ill to kneel to me.
> What is it I can have done to merit this?

---

[66] St Simeon Stylites (circa 388-459) was the first known Christian ascetic "pillar" saint. Early in his life he gained renown for his incredible self-imposed privations, for the power of his preaching, and for many miracles that were attributed to him. In order to escape the crowds and devote himself to God, he began building (circa 423) a succession of stone pillars of ever-increasing height, which finally rose to 20 metres or more. At the top of this lofty pillar Simeon placed a small wooden platform, fully exposed to the elements. There he established himself (circa 439) and spent the last 20 years of his life exercising enormous influence through his preaching (from the top of the pillar), letters, theological writings, and continuing miracles. He wore a heavy iron collar, fasted often and at great length, and was known to prostrate himself before God more than 1,000 times in a single day. See also the *Addendum* – "The Saints of Old," which tells more of Simeon's life, and contains Tennyson's entire poem.

> I am a sinner viler than you all. ...
> It may be I have wrought some miracles,
> And cured some halt and maimed; but what of that?
> It may be, no one, even among the saints,
> May match his pains with mine; but what of that? ...
>
> O my sons, my sons,
> I, Simeon of the pillar, by surname
> Stylites, among men; I, Simeon,
> The watcher on the column till the end;
> I, Simeon, whose brain the sunshine bakes;
> I, whose bald brows in silent hours become
> Unnaturally hoar with rime, do now
> From my high nest of penance here proclaim
> That Pontius and Iscariot by my side
> Showed like fair seraphs. On the coals I lay,
> A vessel full of sin – all hell beneath
> Made me boil over. Devils plucked my sleeve,
> Abaddon and Asmodeus caught at me.
> I smote them with the cross; they swarmed again.
> In bed like monstrous apes they crushed my chest ...

Thus the poet, with remarkable insight, describes the torment of a soul that becomes more wracked with guilt the closer it draws near to God. Indeed, it is doubtful if there has ever been a God-fearing person who has not been sorrowfully aware of sin. The more saintly the soul, the more deeply we expect the servant of God to be filled with contrition for sin, and to shrink back from the immense gulf that lies between a fallen human and a holy God. Saints are honoured for the very fact of their excruciating sense of their sinfulness. We would not consider calling that man a saint who brazenly claimed to be free of sin.

Except Jesus.

Among saints, he alone is known to be a saint because he was free of sin!

Two remarkable things appear here –

First, the example Jesus set in his claim of sinlessness has not caused other good men to pretend to be perfect, but rather, the more they discover the purity of Christ, the more they are driven to deplore their own sin. Far from being offended by his claim, or able to refute it, the most godly minds in every generation have been obliged to acknowledge that Jesus was indeed a man without sin. Thus they admit that while he was truly a man, yet there was in his character an absolute otherness which places him far apart from all other men – he was *"holy, innocent, pure, separate from sinners, (and is now) exalted above the heavens"* (He 7:26).

Which draws me on irresistibly to say –

Second, such a wonderful effect (a sinless man) must have an adequate cause. Who was this man? How came he to be without sin? Is it possible for one who is merely a man to be born without sin? If not, then he must be more than a man!

Indeed, the prophets reckoned the idea of a sinless man was preposterous. Even the angels were known to be tainted with some veniality (Jb 4:18; 15:15).

Absolute impeccability in fact belongs only to God (De 32:4; Ps 18:30; 1 Sa 2:2; Jb 34:10; 36:23; Ps 119:142; 145:17; Ha 1:12,13; Ja 1:13; 1 Jn 1:5; etc.).

Notice how the Lord God himself makes a sharp distinction between himself and humankind on this matter of holiness – *"For I am God and not a human. I am the Holy One in your midst"* (Ho 11:9; and cp. also Nu 23:19). That is also the idea behind Jesus' response to the ruler who asked him – *"Good Teacher, what must I do to inherit eternal life?"* But Jesus said to him – *"Why do you call me good? Only one is good, and that is God!"* (Lu 18:18-19).

The conclusion seems inescapable – if real goodness is solely an attribute of God, then either Jesus was not free from all sin, or he is God.

What do you think?

Chapter Eight

THE GREAT "I AM"

> Jesus was sitting in Moses' chair.
> They brought the trembling woman there.
> Moses commands she be stoned to death.
> What was the sound of Jesus' breath?
> He laid his hand on Moses' law;
> The ancient Heavens in silent awe,
> Writ with curses from pole to pole,
> All away began to roll. [67]

With astonishing boldness Jesus on several occasions countermanded or superseded Moses. [68] How was this possible? How could he dare to speak contrary to the great Lawgiver? He dared, because he was aware of his higher calling and identity. This sense of his deity, as we have seen, probably began to develop in him when he was a boy, and came to fruition in his early manhood. From then on, whether by inference or statement, almost everything Jesus said reflected that awareness. He knew who he was! And he did not hesitate to claim all the attributes and prerogatives that belonged to his divine nature.

Thus, he claimed power over death, a divine authority for his teaching, and, strikingly, to be free from sin. But he went

---

[67] William Blake, The Everlasting Gospel, Section z, lines 7-14; circa 1810. For the gospel story see *John 8:3-11*.

[68] See for example *Matthew 5:21-22, 27-28, 38-39;19:8-9*; etc.

even further. He claimed for himself a prerogative that is entirely divine –

HE CLAIMED AUTHORITY TO FORGIVE SIN

Among the things Jesus did that offended the Jewish religious leaders, hardly anything seemed more shocking than his assertion of the right to forgive sin – see *Mark 2:1-12*. When he told the paralytic that his sins were forgiven, the reaction of the scribes was inevitable – *"Who gave this man the right to say such things? It is blasphemy! Who but God has a right to pardon sin?"* They were angered by the implication that Jesus was himself sinless (for he could hardly offer pardon if he himself needed pardon), and they were furious at his presumption (as it seemed to them) in making himself equal with God.

Notice, Jesus did not contest their claim that only God has the right to forgive sin. He did not argue that they were wrong, that in fact a man *could* offer pardon to a sinner; nor did he soften his actions by saying that he was really only offering the kind of absolution from sin that a priest might do today.

Instead, he went straight into a demonstration, by ridding the man of his paralysis, which showed that he actually did have power to remit sin. Thus he asserted that *his* authority and *God's* authority were one. No wonder the people were amazed, and filled with awe, and went away saying, *"We have seen things today that we hardly dare believe!"* (Lu 5:26).

If I forgive someone, it is assumed that the offender has injured me – I cannot forgive him for hurting someone else. Yet this is what Jesus appeared to do. He perceived that the man had sinned, and that he needed to be assured that his sin was forgiven. But then, instead of counselling the cripple to trust God for pardon (cp. Mi 7:18-20), Jesus pardoned him there and then, thus implying that the Saviour saw himself as the one who had been sinned against. Yet the godly mind acknowledges that all sin is against *God* (Ps 51:4; Ge 39:9; Le 6:2; 2 Sa 12:13) – Jesus thus identified himself with God.

I should once again draw your attention to a matter raised earlier. Notice that the Lord never made any specific claim to be equal with God – at least not in those words. He left his hearers – friends and enemies alike – to draw their own conclusions about the real meaning of what he was saying and doing.

That refusal by Christ plainly to affirm his deity is one of the main proofs used to argue that he must be less than God.

But the argument is shallow. If Christ had known himself to be less than God it is inconceivable that he could have so irresponsibly opened himself to the charge of blasphemy. There was no doubt in the minds of his opponents about the significance of what he was saying. Yet he made no effort either to show them that they had misunderstood him, nor to speak in a way that could not be construed as blasphemous.

On the contrary, his behaviour shows that he accepted the truth of their conclusions (that he was claiming divine prerogatives), but he disallowed their charge of blasphemy. This situation creates an intolerable tension unless the deity of Christ is accepted.

HE CLAIMED TO BE UNIVERSAL JUDGE

Jesus asserted that it would be he who would judge the world (Mt 7:22; 25:31-46), and that the dead would be called from their graves to face the judgment at the sound of *his* voice (Jn 5:25-29).

However, the prophets asserted that the Judge has to be God, for only the Almighty has the wisdom, power, knowledge, and justice to sit upon the Throne of Judgment (De 32:4,35; 1 Ch 16:33; Ps 7:9,11; 9:4,7,8; 50:4,6; 58:11; 96:13; Ec 11:9; 12:14; Is 33:22; etc.). If in fact the Judge who will sit upon that Throne will be Christ, then *he must be identical with God.* The NT writers did not hesitate to make that equation – *Romans 14:10; 2 Corinthians 5:10; Ephesians 6:8-9; Colossians 3:25; 2 Timothy 4:1,8; James 5:9.*

Two objections can be raised against this –

First, it is said that Jesus' authority as Judge is not personal, but delegated to him by the Father (Jn 5:22,27; Mt 11:27; Ac 10:42; 17:31).

Second, the Revelator shows a distinction between God as Judge on the last day, and the Lamb (Re 6:16,17; 11:18; 16:5-7).

The solution to the problem of the relationship that exists between the Father and the Son lies beyond my scope here (it will be discussed in later chapters); but whatever solution is agreed upon, nothing can alter the fact that *the act of judgment requires the use of divine attributes*, and if Christ is to be Judge, then he must possess those attributes. But only deity can possess the special attributes of deity – therefore Christ must be God.

What are these special attributes, which Christ *must* possess if he is to sit upon the throne of judgment? The two that are most prominent are –

- **omnipotence** – for what power less than this could suffice to call all the dead from their graves, and to assemble them before the throne? (Ph 3:20-21; Mt 28:18; Re 1:8,17-18; and notice that the power to give life to the dead is specifically called an attribute of God, Ro 4:17).

- **_omniscience_** – for this work of judgment requires perfect knowledge of all that is good and bad in each person standing there (He 4:13; Jn 2:24-25; 21:17; Ro 2:16; 1 Co 4:5; Re 2:23). But who has that kind of knowledge except God?

Remember also that the work of judgment must be virtually instantaneous for all mankind. It is absurd to imagine each sinner being called to the heavenly bar one after the other, to be tried individually. Even the imagery of a throne, books, spectators, and so on, should probably be seen only as symbols of the fact of judgment.

We have no way of knowing precisely how the judgment will take place. But we can certainly suppose that all people will be judged simultaneously, and that such a universal and instant judgment will require an exercise of limitless knowledge and power. But those two attributes are uniquely properties of the sole God. So once again, if Christ possesses those attributes (and he cannot be Judge without them), he must be God.

HE CLAIMED EQUALITY WITH GOD

> *Jesus made this reply – "My Father keeps on working, and so do I." That is why the Jews were all the more fervent to kill him, because he ... called God his Father, thus making himself equal with God ... "Every one of you," said Jesus, "should honour the Son, just as you should honour the Father. Those who refuse to honour the Son cannot honour the Father who sent him ... The Father is the source of all life, and he has made the Son too to be the source of life." (Jn 5:17-18, 23-26).*

Sayings like those are either blasphemous, as the Jews supposed them to be, or they are simply true. They *would* be blasphemous if the man who spoke them was not equal with the Father. If they *are* true, then the man who spoke them *cannot* be less than the Father in being, even if subordinate in office. [69]

Notice that Jesus did not deny their assumption that he was making himself equal with God. Perhaps more significantly, neither does John, the author of the gospel, deny it. It could perhaps be said that in the heat of the argument, Jesus allowed the opinion of the Jews to stand uncorrected. But that cannot be said of John. It is inconceivable that the apostle would have failed to insert a correction if he knew that the Jews had misunderstood Jesus (cp. 2:21; 7:39; 11:13).

The conclusion is inescapable – John concurred with the opinion of the Jews, that Jesus was claiming equality with God. But who can be equal with God save God?

Consider also the places where Jesus uses the expression *"for my sake"* (Mt 5:11; 10:18; Mk 13:9; Lu 9:24; etc.); and the expression *"for my name's sake"* (Mt 10:22; Mk 13:13; Lu 21:17; Jn 15:21; Ac 9:16; etc.) In the Jewish world of that time, such expressions were quite improper for a man who was only a prophet. A prophet would have said, *"for the Lord's sake,"* or, *"for the name of the Lord."*

Even the holy angels did not dare to command in their own name, nor require that men should serve them or die for their sake (cp. Ju 9). Christ's demand that his disciples

---

[69] Think of your natural father. You are his equal in being and in all essential human attributes; but so long as he lives, he holds a higher office in the family.

should act and speak in his name and for his sake, in the same manner in which the OT saints had acted and spoken in the name of the Lord God, carried a clear inference that he was equal with God.

Psalm 110

Christ's use of *Psalm 110*, linked with quotations from the same Psalm by the apostles, forms a special proof of his equality with God.

Psalm 110 is quoted from or alluded to in the NT more than any other passage from the O.T. [70] Perhaps for this very reason it has received special attention from critical scholars, who have argued that David was not its author, that it is no more than a song eulogising a militant ruler, and the like.

Some of the critical theories have merit, and the scholars have certainly added many colourful insights to the psalm. However, along with most, if not all evangelical scholars, I remain satisfied that David was its author, and that he knew he was writing ultimately about the Messiah. But even if this is not so, nothing can alter the opinion Jesus had about this psalm, nor the way in which it was interpreted by him and by the apostles. The NT clearly shows that Jesus and the apostles found in this psalm a statement both of his messianic identity and of his divinity.

Psalm 110 is an enthronement song, celebrating the crowning of a new sovereign; except that David is addressing

---

[70] Ps 110:1 – see Mt 22:44; 26:64; Mk 12:36; 14:62; 16:19; Lu 20:42-43; 22:69; Ac 2:34-35; Ro 8:34; 1 Co 15:25; Ep 1:20; Cl 3:1; He 1:3,13; 8:1; 10:12,13.
Ps 110:4 – see Jn 12:34; He 5:6,10; 6:20; 7:3,17,21.

a King who is superior to himself. Here is one king doing homage to another greater King –

> So King David ... (delivers) the enthronement oracle to the Messianic King, corresponding to the oracle given to other kings at their anointing or crowning (cp. 1 Sa 10:1 ff.; 2 Kg 11:12). Therefore those who deny David's authorship of the psalm on the grounds that the psalm reads like an enthronement oracle, curiously miss the point.
>
> It is just such an oracle. What is unique is the royal speaker, addressing this more-than-royal person ... The startling fact that David spoke of a king as 'my Lord' ... was pointed out by Christ (Mk 12:35,ff.), who left his hearers to think out its implications, and his apostles to spell them out.
>
> Like Joshua (who surrendered his command with the words, "What does my Lord bid his servant?"), David here (so to speak) falls down and worships the Man who stands before him (cp. Js 5:14). [71]

On the same theme, Albert Barnes writes –

> The phrase "my Lord" refers to someone who was superior in rank to the author of the psalm; one whom he could address as his superior. The psalm, therefore, cannot refer to David

---

[71] Derek Kidner, Psalms 73-150; <u>Tyndale Old Testament Commentaries</u>; General Editor D.J. Wiseman; Intervarsity Press, London, U.K.; pg. 392,393; 1975.

himself, as if Jehovah had said to *him*, "Sit thou at my right hand."

Nor was there anyone on earth in the time of David to whom it could be applicable; anyone whom he would call his "Lord" or superior. If, therefore, the psalm was written by David, it must have reference to the Messiah – to one whom David owned as his superior – his Lord – his Sovereign. It cannot refer to God as if *he* were to have this rule over David, since God himself is referred to as *speaking* to him whom David called his Lord – "Jehovah said unto my Lord." The reasoning of the Saviour, therefore, in *Matthew 22:43-45*, was founded on a fair and just interpretation of the psalm, and was so plain and conclusive that the Pharisees did not attempt to reply to it. [72]

The psalm begins with the words, *"A Psalm of David"* (which in the Hebrew are part of the first line); but the next sentence reads, *"The Lord (Yahweh) says to my Lord (Adonai) ..."* The oracular formula, *"The Lord says ... ,"* is found in the book of Psalms only in this one place. It is a direct claim that what follows is a solemn oracle of God, the words of the Almighty himself. This is the only psalm which makes such an emphatic claim of divine inspiration. Jesus endorsed this when he said that David had written these words when he was *"inspired by the Spirit"* (Mt 22:42ff).

Notice how this dialogue between Christ and the Pharisees presumes two things – *(a)* everyone agreed that the psalm was written by David; *(b)* everyone agreed that the psalm

---

[72] <u>Notes on the Psalms</u>; Vol. 3; Gall and Inglis, London; pg.151; c.1860(?).

was a prophetic oracle about the Messiah. So here is a passage of inspired prophecy, which describes the Messiah as David's *"Lord"* (in contrast with the passages that speak of him as David's son), and which Christ boldly applied to himself.

Thus in one stroke he claimed to be the focus of the prophecy, and to have both human and divine origins. It was a bold stroke!

The sense of Jesus' argument against the Pharisees is this – if the Messiah is both David's son and David's lord, then he must possess both a human and a superhuman nature. The Pharisees, therefore, were in error when they said that any man who claimed to be the Son of God was a blasphemer, because David's words show that an amalgam of human and divine natures *is* indeed possible. Even before Jesus claimed to be the Son of God there were already godly Jews who understood that the Messiah would bear that title (cp. Jn 1:34, 49, where both speakers, recognising that their Messiah was among them, without hesitation called him *"Son of God"*).

Naturally, then, Christ insisted that at least one man, the Messiah, would have to make a claim of divinity when he presented himself to Israel. The Pharisees could perhaps charge Jesus with *delusion* for claiming to be Son of Man and Son of God (that is, the Messiah), but they could not reasonably charge him with *blasphemy*. On the contrary, if he had *not* claimed possession of this double nature, then he would have been instantly exposed as an impostor! As though he had said – *"Even if I am not the Messiah, it still holds that the true Messiah, when he comes, will have to declare himself both David's Lord and David's son – that is, both God and man!"*

Psalm 110:1 declares that the Messiah was already alive in David's time, and that his proper title is *"Adonai"* = "Lord".

While *"Adonai"* is often used in the OT as a term of respect for a magistrate, ruler, master, etc., it is also frequently used of God – eg. *Exodus 4:10,13; 5:22; 15:17*; and many other places, including *verse 5* of our present psalm – *"The Lord is at your right hand."*

The use of the same title in such a short passage – once of God and once of a Person sitting at God's right hand – strongly suggests that this Person possesses an honour which, if it is not fully equal to God's honour, must be little inferior to it. At least it is difficult, in the context of this psalm, to give *"Adonai"* a lesser sense in verse one than it has in verse five. This was certainly the way the apostles understood the matter – eg. *Hebrews 1:3,13*.

HE CLAIMED TO SATISFY

Ask any prophet or priest in ancient Israel, "Who alone can satisfy the deepest needs of man?" and the reply would be instant – *"Only the Lord God can guide and satisfy my soul!"* (Is 58:11; see also, Ps 90:14; 91:16; 36:8-9; 81:16; 103:5; 107:9; Je 31;14; etc.). For another who was less than God to claim the role of Satisfier – whether man or angel – would have been plain blasphemy.

Yet, Jesus, knowing full well what was written in the scriptures, made exactly this claim – *Matthew 11:28-30; John 6:35*. Was he then a blasphemer (as the Jews accused), or is it simply true that <u>Jesus</u> and <u>Yahweh</u> are the same?

HE CLAIMED WORSHIP

If another man allows me to worship him, without rebuking me, then he must be unscrupulous, or mocking me, or deceived by delusions of grandeur – or, *simply deserving worship*. What then was Jesus when he allowed Thomas to address him, *"My Lord and my God!"*? To say that Thomas was only making a colloquial ejaculation (such as, "Good Lord!") would be an insult to both Thomas and the author of the gospel (John). Although some have pressed for that interpretation, it really does not deserve consideration. The passage plainly means what it implies – *Thomas was offering worship to Christ.*

Was Jesus deceived? Was he a blasphemer? Why did he not rebuke Thomas? Why did John not point out that Thomas had committed a grave blunder when he called Jesus *"Lord"* and *"God"*? There is only one answer – Jesus knew that Thomas had spoken the simple truth. It is proper to worship Christ, because to worship him is to worship God.

Thomas, of course, was not the first person to worship Jesus –

> *Those in the boat worshipped him, saying, "Truly you are the Son of God" ... Jesus met them and said, "Hail!" And they came up and took hold of his feet and worshipped him (Mt 14:33; 28:9).*

It is hard for us today to imagine how astonishing such statements are, coming from the pens of Jewish writers, who were sternly monotheistic in their beliefs. The impact of Jesus upon them must have been shattering to enable them to write, without embarrassment, without apology or comment, that they and others had fallen at the feet of Jesus and worshipped him. To a Jew in those days (and indeed today) it would have been impossible to make a more blasphemous statement. The gospel writers are freed from the charge of blasphemy only if it is accepted that Jesus is divine, and thus should be worshipped.

Remember how the early Christians refused to call Caesar *"Lord"* or *"God"*. Rather than speak such blasphemy they preferred to be torn apart by wild beasts, sawn asunder, racked and burnt, and to suffer every kind of hideous torture.

Yet with eager joy they gave those titles and more to the Man of Galilee.

Jesus' calm acceptance of worship should be compared with the reaction of the apostles when the crowd tried to give *them* divine honours. Paul and Barnabas, for example, tore their garments and rushed among the people, begging them to stop (Ac 14:14; see also 3:12ff). Even the holy angels are horrified when anything that resembles worship is offered to them (Re 19:10). If Jesus were less than God, and therefore unfit to be worshipped (Ex 34:14; De 11:16), would he not, like the apostles and the angels, have disclaimed any pretensions to deity?

HE CLAIMED THE TITLE "I AM"

> Tell them, *"I AM,"* Jehovah said
> To Moses; while earth heard in dread,
>   And, smitten to the heart,
> At once above, beneath, around,
> All Nature, without voice or sound,
>   Repli'd, "O Lord, THOU ART."
>
> – Christopher Smart (1722-1771), from *A Song to David*.

At least 25 times in the gospel of John, Jesus used the expression *"I am"* – 6:35, 48, 51; 7:34, 36; 8:12, 18, 23, 24, 28, 58; 10:7, 9, 11, 14; 11:25; 12:26; 14:3, 6; 15:1, 5; 18:5-6, 8, 37. In the Greek text this phrase is very strongly expressed; the first person pronoun is added to the verb to be, to form an emphatic statement – "*I*, even *I* am." Notice –

Normally a Greek verb contains within itself the pronoun that indicates who is speaking. For example, the verb *lego* by itself means "I say"; *estin* means "he is"; *ageis* means "you bring"; and so on. There is no need in Greek to add to these verbs the pronouns "I," "he," or "you," for the pronouns are already included in the verb and are shown by the way the verb is spelled. (73) But an exception to this rule occurs when special emphasis is required; that is, when a person wants to write "*I* say," "*he* is," "*you* bring."

In spoken English, we might create an emphasis by adding to the verb an intensifying pronoun, thus – "I *myself* say," "he *himself* is;" etc. The Greeks achieved the same effect by adding to the verb an ordinary personal pronoun, thus – *Ego lego* – "I, I say;" *Autos estin* – "he, he is;" *Su ageis* – "you, you bring;" and so on.

So the phrase "I am" would normally be just one word in Greek – *eimi*, the nominative singular form of the verb to be. But in the references given above it is emphasised every time by adding the pronoun, thus – *Ego eimi* = "I, I am."

In English, the sense is better conveyed by an expression such as, *"I, yes even I myself, am,"* and the idea is one of exclusiveness – Jesus is not only *"the way, the truth, and the life"* (14:6), but he is the *only* way, the *only* truth, the *only* life. Thus he is also the *only* bread of life, the *only* light of the world, the *only* door of the sheep, and so on. In claims like those, so exclusive, so beyond the scope of any ordinary person, so emphatic, there is an implicit assertion of deity.

Jesus frequently used the Greek pronoun *ego* to emphasise the uniqueness and authority of his teaching – especially when he was giving a new command. Thus, instead of using the ordinary expression *lego* – "I say," he used the emphatic

---

(73) This changing of the grammatical meaning of a word by changing its spelling is called "inflection". Ancient Greek was a highly inflected language, as, long ago, English also used to be. Few of the old inflections remain in English, but some are still common, such as, I *am*, he/she *is*, you *are*; or, I/he/she *was*, we/they/you *were*; or such variations as go, goes, gone, went; or, child/children; or, lie, lied, lay, lain, laid; etc.

formula, *Ego lego* – "I, yes I myself, say ... " (Mt 5:22,28,32,34,39,44; etc.) There is an arrogation of authority in such expressions that is unconscionable if they are less than simply true.

When Jesus spoke of Abraham he said, *"Before Abraham was, I am"* (Jn 8:58). Note that the emphasised pronoun is again used here – *Ego eimi* – "I (yes even I) am." Note also that grammatically it would be better to say, "Before Abraham was, I was." But Jesus chose his words carefully. The expression "I am" implies continuous existence – the kind of existence known only to God. Christ was claiming to have been both pre-existent and continually with the Father, throughout all time.

But perhaps the chief significance of this saying of Jesus is that it corresponds almost exactly to the words spoken by God in *Exodus 3:14*, *"I am who I am"* In fact, the Greek LXX uses the very words *Ego eimi* in *Exodus 3:6,14; 20:2*; etc. They are also found in *Zephaniah 2:15*, where Nineveh, claiming equality with God, boasted, *"I am and there is none else"* – and for this blasphemy the prophet denounced her – *"What a desolation she has become, a lair for wild beasts!"* Against that background, Jesus' use of *Ego eimi* in *John 8:58* can hardly be seen as anything less than a claim of eternal existence and of perfect equality with God.

Commenting on the way Jehovah's Witnesses try to evade this issue, Walter Martin writes:

> ...Jehovah, speaking to Moses, said "I am", which any intelligent scholar recognises as synonymous with God. Jesus literally said to them, "I am Jehovah" (I am), and it is clear that they understood him to mean just that, for they attempted, as the next verse reveals, to stone him.

Hebrew law on this point states five cases in which stoning was legal – and bear in mind that the Jews were legalists. Those cases were – (1) familiar spirits, Le 20:27; (2) Cursing (blasphemy), Le 24:10-23; (3) False prophets who lead to idolatry, De 22:21-24; Le 20:10; (4) Stubborn Son, De 21:18-21; and (5) Adultery or Rape, De 22:21-24; Le 20:10.

Now any honest Bible student must admit that the only legal ground the Jews had for stoning Christ (and actually they had none at all) was the second violation – namely, blasphemy.

Many zealous Jehovah's Witnesses maintain that the Jews were going to stone Jesus because he called them the children of the devil (Jn 8:44). But if this were true, why did they not stone him on other occasions when he called them sons of vipers? (Mt 12:34; 23:33; etc.). The answer is very simple. They could not stone Christ on that ground because they were bound by the law which gives only five cases, and would have condemned them on their own grounds had they used "insult" as a basis for stoning. [74]

William Hendriksen comments on the passage –

Jesus said to them, "I most solemnly assure you, before Abraham was born, I am." The Jews had committed the error of ascribing to Jesus a merely temporal existence. They saw

---

[74] <u>The Kingdom of the Cults</u>; Bethany Fellowship Inc., Minneapolis, Minnesota; revised edition, 1977; pg. 77.

only the historical manifestation, not the eternal Person; only the human, not the divine. Jesus, therefore, reaffirms his eternal, timeless, absolute essence ... Over against Abraham's fleeting span of life (see Ge 25:7) Jesus places his own timeless present ... The "I am" here (8:58) reminds one of the "I am" in 8:24. Basically the same thought is expressed in both passages; namely, that Jesus is God!

The opposition against Jesus (then) reaches a new height. Unable to restrain themselves and their wrathful indignation any longer, and apparently viewing Christ's statement as horrible blasphemy, which must be punished with death by stoning (Le 24:16), the Jews run to a place in the large temple-area where building operations are still being carried on (cp. 2:20) ... Stones are lying all around. These they pick up in order to hurl them at Jesus, thus to put him to death without due process of law or trial by court ...

In the meantime, however, Jesus – knowing, of course, that the proper moment to lay down his life had not yet arrived – hid himself (perhaps amid a crowd of friends) and went out of the temple. [75]

Leon Morris says that the way in which Jesus used *ego eimi* in *John 8:58* is "in the style of deity –

---

[75] New Testament Commentary – *The Gospel of John*; Baker Book House, Grand Rapids, Michigan; 1972; pg. 66, 67 of the second volume.

> It is an emphatic form of speech and one that would not normally be employed in ordinary direct speech. Thus to use it was recognisably to adopt the divine style. In passages like vs. 24, 28 this is fairly plain, but in the present passage it is unmistakable.

Then, showing that eternal continuity is implied in this special use of *eimi*, he quotes Morgan –

> That is a supreme claim to deity; perhaps the most simple and sublime of all the things (Jesus) said with that great formula of old, the great "I AM" ... These are the words of the most impudent blasphemer that ever spoke, or the words of God incarnate. [76]

And he also quotes Stauffer –

> (The "I AM" formula) is Jesus' boldest declaration about himself ... (It) means – where I am, there is God, there God lives, speaks, calls, asks, decides, loves, chooses, forgives, rejects, hardens, suffers, dies. Nothing bolder can be said, or imagined. [77]

> The meaning of the phrase (*ego eimi*) in the sense of full Deity is especially clear at *John 13:19*, where Jesus says he has told them things before they come to pass, that when they do come to pass the disciples may believe that

---

[76] The New International Commentary on the New Testament – *The Gospel According to John*; W.B. Eerdmans Pub. Co., Grand Rapids, Michigan; 1977; pg. 473, 474.

[77] Ibid.

"*Ego eimi*" (I am). Jehovah is the only one who knows the future as a present fact. Jesus is telling them beforehand that when it does come to pass in the future, they may know that "*I am*" ... that is, that he is Jehovah! [78]

CONCLUSION

Jesus may have been a deceiver – making claims that he knew were false; or he may have been mentally deranged – making claims that he thought were true, not realising that they were false. But neither of those theories explains the miracles he wrought, the allegiance he gained from thousands of good people, nor the purity of his life. If he was not mad, if he was not bad, then he must have been true. Jesus passed the two most penetrating tests of character: enmity and intimacy –

HIS ENEMIES COULD FIND NO FAULT IN HIM

They tried very hard to fault him, but without success. They accused him of being demon possessed (Jn 8:48); of blasphemy (Lu 5:21); of breaking the law (Lu 13:14); and so on. But they failed to convict him of sin. None of the charges brought against him was valid (Jn 8:46; and cp. Mt 26:59,ff.).

HIS FRIENDS COULD FIND NO FAULT IN HIM

The impeccable character given to Christ in the gospels might be what we would expect to find, whether or not Jesus was a sinner – except that scripture does not hesitate to record with ruthless honesty the faults of other major

---

[78] Martin, op.cit., pg.78.

characters, such as Moses, David, Elijah, Judas, Peter, Thomas.

A graphic example of biblical honesty is seen in the gospel of *Mark*. This gospel was probably based on Peter's teaching, and it could have been biased in Peter's favour – yet it faithfully records Peter's denial of Christ (14:66, ff.). Nor do his friends praise him (in the gospels, that is). There is an unaffected naturalness in the gospels which is quite surprising. No attempt is made to eulogise Jesus, nor to prove that he was free of sin, nor to argue (as I am doing in this book) that he must have been divine. The four evangelists simply tell what Jesus did. The record itself is sufficient to convince any fair-minded reader that Jesus is all he claimed to be! (Ponder the impact of such passages as *Mark 3:7-12; Luke 8:40-56.*)

Despite their close familiarity with Jesus, their association with him in labour and leisure, at home and in public, their observance of his behaviour when he was adulated and when he was cursed, the disciples were adamant that he was free of sin. They boldly identified him with the King of Righteousness whose coming had been predicted by the prophets –

- the coming of this Righteous Prince is predicted in Psalm 45:7; Isaiah 11:40-5; 32:1; 50:5; 53:9; Zechariah 9:9.5; etc.
- he is identified with Christ in Luke 1:35; Acts 3:14; 4:27,30; 2 Corinthians 5:21; Hebrews 1:9, 4:15, 9:14; 1 Peter 1:19; 2:22; 1 John 2:1; 3:5.

The disciples were greatly daring when they proclaimed the sinlessness of Christ, for that was really an assertion of his divinity. But they offered no apology for the claim, nor any qualification of it. Indeed, they could hardly have been more emphatic. And those who had known Jesus most intimately in the flesh were boldest to declare his innocence. Thus Peter wrote – *"He committed no sin, no guile was found upon his lips;"* and John also – *"Jesus Christ the righteous ... in him there is no sin."*

From that day to this no one has been able to fault the character of Christ. The power of his personality surges from the pages of the gospels today as much as it did in the first century. For many people, just to encounter Christ through reading the gospel stories is a stunning experience; it is hard to imagine what an impact he must have had on those who actually met him in person.

John conveys some idea of what such an encounter meant –

> *The Word became flesh and dwelt among us, full of grace and truth; we beheld his glory, glory as of the only Son from the Father (1:14).*

No wonder multitudes pressed after him! [79]

It is remarkably difficult to portray in literature a character acceptable to every generation. What is commendable in one age is often repulsive in another. For example, many fictional heroes of the 19th century seem merely absurd to modern readers. But the character of Jesus is as compelling today as it has ever been. The gospel writers achieved this literary miracle, not by conscious art, but simply and naturally, because they were just telling the truth. Their Lord was not fictitious; they reported honestly what they had seen and heard.

Who then was this sinless person?

---

[79] Of course, not all did so, for there were many who "loved darkness rather than light, because their deeds were evil" (3:19).

One thing is clear – he was not just a good man. No person who was merely "good" would make the claims Jesus made – if he did, he would cease to be good! Modern society, which likes to eulogise Jesus as a fine example of uprightness and nobility of character – but no more – refuses to face the dishonesty of its attitude toward him. Christ cannot be admired unless all the claims he made about himself are accepted. If those claims are denied, then Jesus must be rejected as a madman, or worse. There is nothing left to admire, and certainly no example to follow.

Since he cannot have been merely a "good man", may we perhaps call him a Son of God – more than a man, but less than God? But as we consider the many claims he made about himself it becomes evident that this is not an adequate explanation, neither for this Man himself, nor for his words and deeds.

So we must press the matter higher. And when we do so, we find ourselves driven to the stunning and awful conclusion that this Man must after all be Emmanuel – *God with us!*

Chapter Nine

ALL THE PROPHETS

> The last and greatest herald of Heaven's King,
> Girt with rough skins, hies to the deserts wild,
> Among that savage brood the woods forth bring,
> Which he more harmless found than man, and mild.
> His food was locusts, and what there doth spring,
> With honey that from virgin hives distill'd;
> Parch'd body, hollow eyes, some uncouth thing
> Made him appear, long since from earth exiled.
> There burst he forth – All ye whose hopes rely
> On God, with me amidst these deserts mourn,
> Repent, repent, and from old errors turn!
> —Who listen'd to his voice, obey'd his cry?
> Only the echoes, which he made relent,
> Rung from their flinty caves, Repent! Repent!
>
> – William Drummond, *St John Baptist* (1585-1649)

What did the prophets say about the Messiah? Do their words agree with his personal claim of deity? Or does that claim represent a radical departure from what the prophets foretold about the coming King of Israel?

The answers to those questions – as we continue our quest for the real identity of Jesus of Nazareth – are the theme of this chapter.

Apart from the claims made by Jesus himself, there is abundant evidence in other scriptures that full deity must be ascribed to him. But first, it is fair to say that nowhere in the Bible is the deity of Christ stated formally, as a developed doctrine. The prophets, of course, could hardly be expected to have possessed an unclouded vision of the coming

Deliverer. But what about the apostles? As it happens, they too did not attempt to systemise or formalise their ideas about the nature of Christ (as, say, Paul did with his doctrine of justification by faith). The formalising of our present doctrine of the Godhead (as later chapters will show) is rather the product of the labour of many thinkers across many centuries.

That does not make the doctrine uncertain; for beyond question, the OT has many statements that ascribe the glory of the Lord God himself to the Messiah who was to come. Likewise, the NT is full of expressions that show how, from the beginning, the early church thought of Christ in terms of deity. In this, of course, the apostles were simply reflecting the inevitable meaning of Christ's own claims, and they were also responding to the plain statements of the OT prophets. The apostolic witness will be taken up in the second volume of this study (the first chapter). Here we want to look at –

THE WITNESS OF THE PROPHETS

ISAIAH 9:6

The titles of the Messiah are – *Wonderful, Counsellor, Mighty God, Everlasting Father, Prince of Peace.* Opponents of the deity of Christ have tried to argue that the Hebrew words translated *Mighty God* ("El Gibbor") can also be translated *"Powerful Magistrate," "Mighty Ruler,"* or *"Strong Hero,"* and that (it is said) is how they should be rendered here.

To that argument we can raise two objections. *First*, the Hebrew word *El* is nowhere else used by Isaiah to refer to anyone other than the Lord God. *Second*, the phrase *El Gibbor* is used by Isaiah in the very next chapter as a name for God – *"A remnant will return ... to the Mighty God"* (10:21). It is improbable that the prophet would have used such a significant phrase twice in such proximity, and yet intend it to mean something different each time. If *El Gibbor* is the *Mighty God* in 10:21, then he must also be the *Mighty God* in 9:6.

The same phrase, although in a slightly different form, can be found in *Deuteronomy 10:17; Nehemiah 9:32; Psalm 24:8*. Each of those references pre-dates Isaiah. He was familiar with them. When he spoke of the Son who would be given to Israel, and called him *Mighty God*, he must have seen that in some mysterious way this Son would be the same as he of whom Moses had said – *"The Lord your God is God of gods and Lord of lords, the great, the mighty, and the terrible God."*

Another variation of *El Gibbor* was used by Jeremiah (32:18); yet he would have been familiar with Isaiah's oracle and cautious about applying this title to God if there were any doubt concerning its meaning.

Names in Hebrew were more than just titles or identifiers; they were intended to express the character of those who bore them. When Isaiah called the Child *Mighty God* and *Everlasting Father*, he was giving him the nature and attributes of deity; he was announcing that God would be on earth in the person of this Son.

ISAIAH 7:14

> ... *a young woman shall conceive and bear a son, and shall call his name Emmanuel.*

Commentators and translators differ as to whether the Hebrew word *almah* should be translated *young woman* or *virgin*; they also disagree about whether this woman was Isaiah's wife, or another woman; and they debate whether or not the boy *Emmanuel* was the prophet's son, or the baby prince Hezekiah, or another; and about whether the prophecy had a contemporary fulfilment in Isaiah's time, or refers exclusively to Christ!

I am inclined to believe that the *almah* was the prophet's wife, and *Emmanuel* was one of the two symbolic names given to Isaiah's second son (cp. 8:1,ff.), and that the prophecy did have a contemporary fulfilment in the lifetime of this boy – at least that appears to me to be the best sense of the whole passage (7:1-8:18).

However, whatever contemporary meaning the oracle may have had, it is impossible to deny that Isaiah himself saw a future and much more significant fulfilment, and that his wife and son were only symbols of another Almah and Son who would one day appear in Israel. The prophecies are all carefully phrased, to allow for both the lesser and greater fulfilment.

That the first boy to be called *Emmanuel* would be born and live during the years immediately following Isaiah's encounter with Ahaz, seems clear from his words in 7:8b, and vs. 15-17.

But that the real *Emmanuel* was a Person much greater than any son of Isaiah's could be, seems to be equally clear from the prophet's other references to him in 8:8, 10; and by his magnificent oracle about the Son in 9:6.

The translators of the LXX (who wrote some 500 years after Isaiah) apparently felt this way; for they chose the Greek word *parthenos* to translate the Hebrew *almah*. Now *almah* may mean either a virgin, or a young woman (whether married or not); therefore it could be applied to Isaiah's wife. But *parthenos* can only mean an *unmarried virgin*. But is *parthenos* a good substitute for *almah*? Matthew obviously thought so, since he agreed with the Greek translators, and copied them in his famous quote – "*Behold, a virgin* (parthenos) *shall conceive and bear a son, and his name shall be called Emmanuel*" (1:23).

Whether or not Matthew thought the prophecy had already had an initial fulfilment in the time of Isaiah, he plainly believed that in its *deeper* meaning it was not fulfilled until Christ was born. Also, by his use of *parthenos*, Matthew showed his belief that the true fulfilment of the prophecy required a *virgin woman* to conceive a child supernaturally. That Child would be the promised Messiah, who would truly (not symbolically) be *Emmanuel ... God-With-Us*.

The implicit supernatural character of the oracle, which lifts it above a merely local or contemporary fulfilment, is pointed out by E.J. Young –

> The birth of the child is to be a sign. It is true that in itself a sign need not be a miracle; but in this particular context, after the command issued to Ahaz to ask for a sign deep or high, one would be justified in expecting a sign such as the recession of the shadow on the sundial. There should be something unusual in the birth; a birth in the ordinary course of nature would not seem to meet the requirements of the sign.

Dr Young goes on to argue that *almah* must refer to a young unmarried woman; then he comments –

> This unmarried woman might have been immoral, in which case the birth could hardly have been a sign. We are left then with the conclusion that the mother was a good woman

and yet unmarried; in other words, the birth was supernatural. [80]

Because other factors in the full prophecy introduce an element of ambiguity, and seem to require at least a partial fulfilment in Isaiah's own time, I disagree with Dr Young's claim that the *Emmanuel* oracle refers exclusively to Christ. But I do agree that the way Isaiah has expressed himself does demand an ultimate and supernatural fulfilment of his vision. In that final realisation of the oracle, the Messiah is born of a virgin, and in him the fulness of God is to dwell bodily (cp. Cl 2:9).

> It means what it says, God is with us. A mortal body, a human soul, became for a little while the habitation of the Spirit of God. It is a stupendous and almost inconceivable thought ... (To) sober reason the thought of God dwelling among us is not easy. Yet daring as it is, there is something about God and something about man which make such a coming of the divine not incredible, but indeed almost inevitable –
>
> "<u>Something about God</u>." If God is a person, we would expect that he would make himself known. If he is indeed Love, nothing could keep him from his children. The Incarnation becomes a necessity. Therefore God took the one way in which to reveal his love – he became one of us. Through the life of Jesus Christ he spoke to us by human lips, and

---

[80] <u>The New Bible Dictionary</u>, art. "Emmanuel"; The Intervarsity Fellowship, London; 1967; pg.556.

looked on us with human eyes. It is of him and him alone that we may say, Emmanuel, God is with us.

"Something about man." A son of Adam he may be, a frail and sinful creature, but a son of God too, with a capacity for faith and eternal things, an unquenchable spark of the divine in him, so that we dare to say that he is 'made in the image of God.' Surely that fact justifies his right to hope that the yearnings of his soul for knowledge of God would finally be answered. It is not reasonable to think that God created us for himself only to mock us. J.D. Jones once said, 'An instinct is an argument, and a desire is equal to a demonstration.' ... (So) 'the Word was made flesh, and dwelt among us' (Jn 1:14)." [81]

YAHWEH IS JESUS

There are numerous references to "Yahweh" in the OT which in the NT are specifically applied to "Jesus" – thus proving that the apostles made no distinction between the two. But *Yahweh* is the personal covenant name of *God* – therefore Jesus is God.

The "Yahweh" references fall into the following groups –

"THE DAY OF THE LORD"

There are several places where the NT writers refer to *"the day of Christ"* (1 Co 5:5; 2 Co 1:14; Ph 1:6; 1 Th 5:2; 2 Pe

---

[81] GGD Kilpatrick, in his "Exposition", in loc., The Interpreter's Bible, Vol. 5; Abingdon Press, New York; 1956; pg. 218, 219.

3:10,12). Notice how this *"day of Christ"* is directly linked with similar OT references that refer to *"the day of Yahweh"* (Is 13:9-10; Jl 1:15; 2:11,31; 3:14; Zp 1:67,14; Je 45:10; Mal 4:5; etc).

Such a substitution of *"the day of Jesus"* for *"the day of God"* would have been unthinkable, unless the NT writers had identified Christ with God.

"YAHWEH" REFERENCES THAT ARE APPLIED TO CHRIST

Compare the following –

- Isaiah 40:3 with Matthew 3:3
- Psalm 68:18 with Ephesians 4:7-8
- Psalm 102:26 with Hebrews 1:10-11
- Joel 2:32 with Romans 10:13
- Isaiah 45:21-23 with Philippians 2:10-11

NT REFERENCES TO JESUS THAT ECHO OT REFERENCES TO YAHWEH

Compare the following –

- Psalm 23:1 with John 10:11
- Isaiah 44:6 with Revelation 1:8,17-18; 2:8; 22:12-13
- Zechariah 14:1,3-4 with Acts 1:11-12; etc
- Isaiah 8:13 with 1 Peter 3:15
- Genesis 4:26; 12:8 with Romans 10:12; 1 Corinthians 1:2

Perhaps the most striking example of NT writers taking hold of OT terms and applying them to Christ is found in the *Apocalypse*. Thus, C. Anderson Scott writes –

> ... the Apocalypse of John ... represents the Christology of the primitive community, not developed by intellectual analysis ... (yet) in no

book in the NT do devotion to, and adoration of Christ, and recognition of his participation in the glory and authority of the Father, find such copious, such exalted, expression.

Yet the forms in which this expression is cast are for the most part not original ... the OT has been laid under contribution ... Attributes and functions, descriptions and imagery which had played their part in setting forth the majesty and the almighty power of God, are gathered from all available sources and attached to the Person of the heavenly Christ ...

Divine titles are ascribed to him, as 'Lord of lords, and King of kings' (17:14; 19:16); and Divine functions, in the searching of the heart and reins (2:23; cf. Ps. 7:9); and a share both in the throne of God (22:1), and in the worship paid to God, even the worship paid by angels (5:11). He holds the keys of Hades and of death (1:18), which according to Jewish tradition was one of the prerogatives of the Almighty. It is before his wrath that men are to tremble in the Day of Judgment (6:16,17) ... The throne on which he has taken his place is his Father's throne (3:21) ... [82]

THE USE OF "LORD" AS AN EQUIVALENT OF "YAHWEH"

No one today knows just how the ancient Hebrews pronounced the name of God. The Hebrew text contains only

---

[82] Hastings, op.cit., vol.3, pg.185.

the four consonants YHWH – known as the *tetragrammaton*. The pronunciation of the *tetragrammaton* has been forgotten, because the Jews held it in such reverence they refused to say it. Whenever they had to read the scriptures aloud, they changed YHWH into the Hebrew word for "Lord" = "Adonai." The *tetragrammaton* has become anglicised as either "Jehovah", or more correctly, "Yahweh;" but many English translations still follow the Jewish practice of substituting "Lord" for the divine Name. [83]

The writers of the NT were familiar with the Greek (LXX) translation of the OT – they quote from it frequently – so they were accustomed to addressing God as "Lord" = *Kyrios* in Greek. There are a number of places where *Kyrios* is used specifically of God (Mt 1:20,22; 5:33; 9:38; 11:25; Ac 2:20,34; 3:19; 4:26; Ro 9:28,29; 12:19; 2 Co 6:16; and there are many other examples).

In each of those places *Kyrios* is used as an analogue of *Yahweh*, and that was a standard way of addressing God in Greek. But then the same writers, without qualification or explanation, use exactly the same form of address for Christ, and do so in the most solemn manner (Ac 2:21; 9:10,13; 10:36; 11:23; and many others.)

Perhaps the most remarkable examples are those places where *Kyrios* is used in the same passage of both God and Christ, and in such a way that it may remain doubtful whether the reference is to God, or Christ, or both. For an example, note the occurrences of *Lord* in *Acts chapters*

---

[83] The RSV follows the practice of the Authorised Version, and translates YHWH as LORD (printed in capitals). A full explanation of this is given in the Preface of the RSV. Most other translations also explain in their preface or introduction the policy followed in translating the various Hebrew names of God.

13,14,15. Again, many other examples could be cited, but it would be tedious to list them all. A search through your concordance will quickly locate them for you. [84]

It is difficult to see how the NT writers could have interchanged *Kyrios* between God and Christ in this manner unless they were convinced that no blasphemy was involved – that is, they were willing to give Christ equal honour with God. *Acts 13:2* is particularly striking – *"While they were worshipping the Lord and fasting ..."* It is uncertain here whether *"Lord"* refers to Christ or God. But that very ambiguity, which evidently did not disturb the early church, shows that for them worship could be directed as readily to the Son as to the Father.

Yet to worship anyone who is less than God is idolatry. Since, then, they were able to worship either Christ or God, without making themselves idolaters, Christ must be one with God.

Another remarkable interchange of *Kyrios* between Christ and God can be seen in Paul's letter to the Thessalonians –

- In *1 Thessalonians 5:23* he writes – "May *God himself, the God of peace*, sanctify you wholly ... at the coming of our Lord Jesus Christ." But then, in *2 Thessalonians 3:16*, he writes – "Now may the *Lord of peace* himself give you peace ... the *Lord* be with you all." Notice – "The *God* of peace ... the *Lord* of peace ... the *Lord*." It is difficult to see how Paul could have used such expressions unless Christ and God were in some way fused together in his mind, so that he saw Christ and God as deserving equal honour.

---

[84] In the KJV, all but 12 occurrences of "Lord" are *Kyrios*; the remaining 12 are divided between *despotes* (10) and *rabboni* (2).

- In *1 Thessalonians 1:4* he uses the phrase "brethren beloved by *God*;" but in *2 Thessalonians 2:13* he changes it to "brethren beloved by the *Lord* (Christ)." There is no indication that it is a lesser thing to be loved by Christ than by God. On the contrary, in both places the expression *"loved by ..."* conveys a sense of highest privilege, of unassailable joy, of infinite grace. To be loved by Christ is a wonder no less immense, a benefit no less eternal, than to be loved by God.

You would not find it difficult, searching through your NT, to find many similar parallelisms – that is, places where *"God"* could be substituted for *"Christ"*, and vice versa, without either diminishing or increasing the strength of the statements. [85]

That kind of ambiguity is inconceivable, and would certainly be blasphemous, unless the writers were convinced that the interchange added nothing to Christ nor took anything from God.

THE CHURCH AND THE CAESARS

THE CULT OF THE EMPEROR

The refusal of the early Christians to pronounce the formula *"Caesar is Lord"* provides a dramatic illustration of the real meaning of the saying *"Jesus is Lord"*. Christians were horribly tortured and relentlessly persecuted for their refusal to praise the emperor as *Kyrios* of the realm. Latourette writes –

---

[85] See the list provided by my brother Dr Barry Chant in the *Addendum*, "Christ the Lord".

Outstanding among the officially supported cults (in the Roman Empire) was that of the Emperor. The East had long been familiar with a ruler who was also a divinity. Alexander the Great had been accorded that role, as had many another potentate in the Orient. It was natural that Augustus, who had brought peace to the distraught Mediterranean world, should be hailed as an incarnation of divinity. Statues of him were erected and religious ceremonies were instituted for him.

An imperial cult followed. It might call forth little personal devotion. However, it was regarded as a safeguard of law and order and important for the preservation and prosperity of the realm. Dissent from it might well be seen as treasonable and anarchistic ... Christians were hauled before the courts as transgressors of the laws ... Since they would not share in the religious rites associated with the imperial cult they were viewed as hostile to the state.

The antagonism was particularly marked, since Christians, revering Christ as *Kyrios*, or Lord of the whole earth, often looked upon the Emperor, for whom the same claim was made, as Anti-Christ, while the imperial authorities were hostile to them as those who gave allegiance to a rival of the Emperor." [86]

Elsewhere, Latourette writes –

---

[86]   K.S. Latourette, A History of Christianity, Vol. 1, *Beginnings To 1500*; Harper and Row, New York; revised edition 1975; pg. 23,24,84; emphasis mine.

> (To promote this emperor cult) temples were erected, not only in Rome itself, but in the many cities of the Empire. The shrines were among the public buildings, and their construction, adornment, and maintenance were matters of civic pride. In the provinces the upkeep of the temples and the celebration of the ceremonies of the cult of Rome were especially the charge of the aristocracy and of the official classes who prided themselves on their Roman citizenship and upon whom fell the burden of civic duties.
>
> The ruling classes looked upon them as an integral part of the established order, and regarded any attack upon them or any refusal to endorse them as a threat to the very existence of the state and of society. It was this conviction ... which gave rise to the most severe persecutions which Christianity encountered." [87]

On the same theme, W.D. Niven writes –

> It is to be noted that it was no mere flattery that was expressed in this deification (of the Roman emperors). It was a sincere sentiment of gratitude that led the East to confer on Caesar the highest honour conceivable. The 'pax Romana' which he gave them and preserved for them was an inestimable boon. He did for them what their gods seemed unable

---

[87] K.S. Latourette, A History of the Expansion of Christianity, Vol. 1, *The First Five Centuries*; Zondervan Publishing House, Grand Rapids, Michigan; 1978; pg. 15.

to do; he put an end to their constant dread and frequent experience of warfare, tyranny, injustice.

He gave them security of life and goods, kept safe the highways, fostered their commerce, and developed their resources. And all those benefits were safeguarded to them by a might which seemed invincible and irresistible ...

Thus we see that deification was an honour spontaneously offered to Caesar by grateful, enthusiastic, and devoted subjects ... (It) may be that the practical mind of a Roman did honestly feel that there was something embarrassing, ludicrous, or even impious in his own deification.

But the same practical mind, with its genius for government, soon perceived that in Caesar-worship the Empire would secure what it lacked – a bond of unity and a powerful safeguard of loyalty ...

Hence Caesar-worship rapidly became organised and highly developed as the State-religion of the Empire; the Caesars so far conquered their reluctance to pose as gods that Domitian proudly designated himself as 'Dominus et Deus', 'Lord and God'. Caesar-worship was enforced by the whole might of the State; refusal to worship the Emperor was high treason. [88]

---

[88] Article, "Emperor Worship;" Hastings, op.cit., Vol. 3; pg. 330-333.

Niven also notes that the early Christians took hold of the language of the imperial cult, and made it their own. He comments –

> To seize as eminently suitable for their own purpose the whole vocabulary of Caesar-adoration was a bold and brilliant stroke of policy on the part of the preachers of Christianity. The humble missionaries, speaking of Jesus as the Emperor was spoken of, must have made a startling and very profound impression. [89]

A DECLARATION OF DEITY

Thus terms that today are exclusively applied to Christ, were in those days universally applied to the Emperor, and were part of the common language of the Roman cult. Throughout the Empire, Caesar was acclaimed, and worshipped, as *"Saviour ... Prince of Peace ... Lord ... Son of God ... Image of God ... Revealed God"* – and the like.

> So when the decree went out that every citizen of the Empire had to offer worship to Caesar, and to receive an official certificate of religious orthodoxy, the Christians resolutely refused. Even when the demand was simplified merely to burning a pinch of incense in a brazier, and saying, "Caesar is Lord," they still refused, for the whole world knew that the formula *Caesar is Lord* actually meant *Caesar is God*. No true Christian could be persuaded to speak such blasphemy; so thousands of them perished in

---

[89] Ibid.

the dungeons and torture chambers of Rome. (90)

They suffered the most agonising torments because, knowing that Caesar was not divine, they adamantly refused to call him "*Lord*" ("*Kyrios*"). Yet those same people went to their deaths crying out again and again, "*Jesus is Lord! Jesus is Lord!*" (cp. Ac 2:36; 1 Co 12:3). But if it is blasphemy to say "*Caesar* is Lord" unless Caesar is God, then it is equally blasphemous to say "*Jesus* is Lord" unless Jesus is God!

The conclusion is inescapable – every person who acclaimed Christ as Lord and Saviour, every martyr who whispered with his dying breath that he had no Lord but Jesus, affirmed, *and knew that he was affirming*, the deity of Christ. No other meaning can be placed on the way the NT

---

(90) The certificates were called *libelli*, and every inhabitant of the empire was required to obtain one, in order to demonstrate loyalty to Caesar. This particular form of oppression was introduced throughout the empire during the reign of Decius (249-251). But Decius was merely the first emperor to institute an empire-wide persecution. The church had already been in conflict with the cult of emperor-worship for 150 years, although actual physical persecution had, until this time, been localised and sporadic. However, it was nonetheless bitter, and many thousands of people had already lost their lives for Christ. The *libellus* certified that its holder had performed the requisite ceremony in the presence of the proper government officials and other witnesses. I have read somewhere that about 40 copies still exist, some only in fragments. The *Encyclopedia Britannica* says about them – "... several papyri survive of the *libelli* submitted in the first official state-sponsored persecution of Christians, under the emperor Decius (ruled 249–251) – these were certificates in which people swore that they had performed sacrifices to pagan gods in order to prove that they were not Christians." (Article "Egypt" in the 2005 online premium edition.)

writers and the early Christians used *Kyrios* in relation to Christ. [91]

The next three chapters offer some practical applications of the doctrine of the absolute pre-eminence of Christ as Son of Man and Son of God.

---

[91] *Kyrios* in the NT, of course, is not always used as a designation of deity. In the Greek language *kyrios* was also a term of respect, implying varying degrees of honour, depending upon who was being addressed – Mt 13:27; 20:8; Ac 25:26; etc. The point of the above argument is that when *kyrios* is applied to Christ, the context, the way in which the term is used, shows that the highest possible honour is being given to him. *Kyrios* in NT usage identifies Jesus with Yahweh, and places him equal with God.

Chapter Ten

THE PRE-EMINENT CHRIST

Christ is the express image of the invisible God. He has sovereign rights over the entire creation. By him everything in heaven and on earth was created, whether they are visible or invisible, or thrones or kingdoms or rulers or powers – whatever exists has been created through him and for him. He himself was before all things, and everything holds together in him. He is the Head of his Body, the church; he is the beginning of the new creation, the first to rise from the dead, so that in everything he might have absolute pre-eminence. (Cl 1:15-18).

The church at Colosse was being troubled by two heresies, both of which have been resurrected in our time –

- **_Legalism_** – that is, the imposition of a set of rules as an essential part of the process of salvation (that is, you must do this or not do that, before you can consider yourself "saved" – see Cl 2:16-23). Human merit, said they, based upon good works, must be added to the work of Christ in order to be securely saved.

- **_Gnosticism_** – that is, the imposition of many layers of demigods between us and Christ. Gnostics [92]

---

[92] The name comes from the Greek word for "knowledge" – *gnosis*.

claimed, like some New Age followers today, to possess special knowledge about the spiritual world.

But Paul would have none of it. He insisted upon the **sufficiency** and **supremacy** of Christ and Christ alone. No rule-keeping could add to the full salvation Christ has wrought for us. No divinities of any sort could interpose themselves between the believer and Christ..

But this was too simple for the Gnostics. They restlessly craved more and more esoteric knowledge about the layered hosts of hidden demi-gods. They yearned to know just what sphere of influence each spiritual ruler had. In their view, malign spirits and beneficent ones alike, could be propitiated and turned into allies. By knowing each power's name and function, and by discovering the correct ritual, supernatural help could be secured. The spirits were more powerful on some days than others; certain seasons were auspicious while others had to be avoided. Each authority had power to prosper or hinder different human enterprises; certain foods and drinks had to be avoided at particular times, and taken at other times. Some things were altogether taboo; others were equally essential.

The Gnostic body of secret lore became ever more ponderous, posing an increasingly impenetrable barrier between the struggling worshipper and God.

Such nonsense was anathema to Paul, who exalted Christ to the highest heaven, driving out every other imaginable intermediary, while yet insisting that the gospel brings Christ into the closest possible bond with the humblest believer.

Let us discover then what Paul meant by his powerful declaration – *"Christ must have pre-eminence in everything!"*

CHRIST is PRE-EMINENT OVER ALL DEITIES

One of the down-sides of our multicultural experiment is a growing multi-religious spectrum. For example, in 1993 nearly 8000 people attended a *Parliament of World Religions* in Chicago. Among the delegates, along with Christians, Jews, Muslims, Hindus, Buddhists, were Baha'is, and devotees of the Fellowship of Isis, the Covenant of the Goddess, the Earth Goddess, the Lyceum of the Venus of Healing, and other cults, ancient and modern. All were claiming the right to an equal place in the sun.

As a consequence, Christians are coming under an increasing pressure toward religious syncretism; that is, people are demanding that we abandon all claim of exclusivity and admit that Christianity is only one of countless pathways to salvation and God, and that we allow the infusion of many other faiths into ours.

Two main factors are empowering this pressure –

- loss of vitality in the church; and
- despair at the condition of the world – its surging population growth; ecological decay; collapsing agriculture; climate change; along with the failure of materialism to bring Utopia; bewilderment in politics, and the nightmare of continuing religious hatreds. [93]

---

[93] The first such Parliament was held in 1893, at which a young Hindu, Swami Vivekananda, greeted Americans as his "brothers and sisters" and caused a sensation by a powerful speech, which included the words – "I fervently hope that the bell that tolled this morning in honour of this occasion may be the death knell of all fanaticism, of all persecutions with the sword or with the pen, and
– continued on next page

But we dare not compromise. We cannot but stand firm in the truth of the gospel (1 Ti 2:5; Ac 4:12; 1 Jn 5:21).

Yet why should we do this? What gives us the right to say that the Christian faith alone is wholly true? *Answer* – the resurrection of Jesus Christ from the dead and his ascension to the Father's right hand. If he has indeed risen from the dead, if he does indeed now sit *"at the right hand of the Majesty on High"* (He 1:4), then all else in heaven, on earth, and below the earth must bow the knee and acknowledge him as Lord (Ph 2:9-11). Which leads to our second affirmation –

CHRIST is PRE-EMINENT OVER ALL DARKNESS

The Father rescued us from the authority of darkness and carried us into the kingdom of his dearly loved Son (Cl 1:13).

HE CONQUERED THE DARKNESS OF DEATH

In the entertainments of the rich among them (the Egyptians), when they have finished eating, a man bears round a wooden figure of a dead body in a coffin, made as like the reality as may be both by painting and carving, and measuring about a cubit or two cubits each way; and this he shows to each of those who are drinking together, saying – "When thou lookest upon this, drink and be merry, for thou shalt be

---

of all uncharitable feelings between persons wending their way to the same goal." (<u>Christian Century</u>, Sep 22-29, 1993; pg. 886.)

such as this when thou art dead." Thus they do at their carousals. (94)

Sobered by the reminder of their mortality, says Herodotus, the tardy guests soon lost interest in the party and went home.

Nothing in life is so harsh and full of dread as the certainty of death. How many times I have stood at my mother's grave, or that of my baby son, struggling to grapple with, to comprehend, the mystery and finality of death! How difficult to ponder the horror of decay that lies in that grave, the utter ruin of all beauty, laughter, love, and life.

Almost every day I must drive at least once or twice past a cemetery on my way to and from home. How hard it is to get some sense of what it will be like when, in a few years, I too must lie there, beneath the hard stone and the cold earth!

How shall we view death? How shall we cope with it?

I did some research and collected some graveyard epitaphs that show a wide span of responses, from humorous defiance to utter despair –

- From an American cemetery, an epitaph quoting scripture to honour a cook. She had served a family faithfully for many years until she fell into the kitchen fire and was burned to death. Her epitaph said –

    Well done, good and faithful servant.

- From a church graveyard in England, an 18th cent. epitaph to a clergyman who died after his horse had bitten him -

---

(94)   The History, by Greek historian Herodotus (c. BC 480-420); tr. GC Macaulay c. 1900; Bk. II, Ch. 78.

> The steed bit his master;
> How came this to pass?
> He heard the good pastor
> Cry, "All flesh is grass!" [95]

- Another one from England –

  > Here lies my wife; here let her lie./
  > Now she's at rest, and so am I.

- One whose location I don't know –

  > Here lies the body of Michael Shay,
  > Who died maintaining his right of way.
  > His case was clear and his will was strong—
  > But he's as dead as if he'd been wrong.

- From an American headstone, in memory of a dentist –

  > Stranger, approach this spot with gravity,
  > John Black is filling his last cavity.

- Back to the British Isles, and an epitaph composed by his friends for a man who had drowned in the River Leith. They should have given more attention to punctuation –

  > Erected to the memory of John McFarlane.
  > Drowned in the water of Leith
  > By a few affectionate friends.

- From the same country, a rather morbid epitaph by a man who wanted to take revenge on the living –

  > Your eyes drop out and your teeth fall in,
  > And the worms crawl over your mouth and chin;

---

[95] Isaiah 40:6.

They invite their friends and their friends' friends too,
And you look like hell when they're through with you!

- A similar one from another person who was determined to put a cloud of doom over everyone who passed by his grave –

    Over us silent dead you need not sigh;
    Rather weep for yourself who dread to die.

- And another from England, composed by a man who saw that death was the great leveller, removing all distinction of rank –

    Nobles and heralds, by your leave,
    Here lies what once was Matthew Prior,
    The son of Adam and of Eve;
    Can prince or pope claim higher?

- Now two or three from ancient Greece, from people who died about the same time the apostles first began to preach the gospel – [96]

    Here lies Callicratia
    Who bore 29 children
    Saw none of them die
    Lived 105 years
    And never once used a walking stick!

    ***

    At 60 I, Dionysios of Tarsus
    Lie here -
    Not having married
    And wishing my father hadn't.

---

[96] Taken from The Greek Anthology, ed. Peter Jay; Penguin Books, 1981.

***

How was I born, and for what purpose?
Why did I come here, only to leave again?
Why learn anything, to end up knowing nothing?

I was born from nothing, and now I am again as I was.
I was not – I was born – I was
And now I am not.
That is all.
Anything else you may say is a lie.
I shall not be again.

So there is mixture of responses to death. In the end they are all made void by the greatest epitaph of all, the one spoken by the angels over the empty tomb of Jesus. He had risen from the dead, and when his disciples came to the burial to see what had happened they were greeted by the angel who said –

"HE IS NOT HERE! HE IS RISEN!"

So the unshakeable foundation upon which the Christian faith stands is the fact of Christ's triumph over the grave. No other faith offers such a Saviour, who became one of us, then smashed our greatest foe!

HE CONQUERED THE DARKNESS OF DESPAIR

One of the very greatest of English poets was John Keats, who died in Rome in 1821 when he was only 26 years old. He left instructions that his name should not be on his headstone, but only the words – "Here lies one whose name was writ on water."

Keats recognised the ephemerality of life, and that even the most renowned man or woman must eventually be forgotten, as Shelley also attests in one his poems –

> I met a traveller from an antique land
> Who said – Two vast and trunkless legs of stone
> Stand in the desert... Near them, on the sand,
> Half sunk, a shattered visage lies, whose frown,
> And wrinkled lip, and sneer of cold command,
> Tell that its sculptor well those passions read
> Which still survive, stamped on these lifeless things,
> The hand that mocked them, and the heart that fed;
> And on the pedestal these words appear –
> "My name is Ozymandias, king of kings –
> Look on my works, ye Mighty, and despair!"
> Nothing beside remains. Round the decay
> Of that colossal wreck, boundless and bare
> The lone and level sands stretch far away. [97]

Indeed, most of us have to accept the demeaning truth that we will be sooner rather than later banished from memory! Will anyone know about you, or care, a hundred years from now?

> Let us drink and be merry, dance, joke, and rejoice,
> With claret and sherry, theorbo and voice!
> The changeable world to our joy is unjust,
> All treasure's uncertain,
> Then down with your dust!
> In frolics dispose your pounds, shillings, and pence,
> For we shall be nothing a hundred years hence.
>
> We'll sport and be free with Moll, Betty, and Dolly,
> Have oysters and lobsters to cure melancholy:

---

[97] Percy Bysshe Shelley (1792-1822), Ozymandias. The traveller in Egypt saw the remains of a huge statue of Ramses II (1279–13 BC. The inscription, once intended as a boast, now becomes an ironic mockery of all the king's former splendour.

Fish-dinners will make a man spring like a flea,
Dame Venus, love's lady,
Was born of the sea;
With her and with Bacchus we'll tickle the sense,
For we shall be past it a hundred years hence.

Your most beautiful bride who with garlands is crown'd
And kills with each glance as she treads on the ground,
Whose lightness and brightness doth shine in such splendour
That none but the stars
Are thought fit to attend her,
Though now she be pleasant and sweet to the sense,
Will be damnable mouldy a hundred years hence.

Then why should we turmoil in cares and in fears,
Turn all our tranquill'ty to sighs and to tears?
Let 's eat, drink, and play till the worms do corrupt us,
'Tis certain, *Post mortem*
Nulla voluptas. [98]
For health, wealth and beauty, wit, learning and sense,
Must all come to nothing a hundred years hence! [99]

So we carry a three-fold burden –

- the memory of past failure
- the necessity for present toil

---

[98] *Post mortem nulla voluptas* means, After death, there will be no more pleasure.

[99] *Coronemus nos Rosis Antequam Marcescant* – Thomas Jordan (1612?–1685). Arthur Quiller-Crouch, ed., The Oxford Book of English Verse, 1919. The title comes from the the Latin version of the apocryphal *Wisdom of Solomon 2:8* – "Let us crown ourselves with roses, before they wither away!"

- the hopelessness of the lifeless grave.

Into that darkness of guilt and futility comes the passionate grace of God in Christ – "You, who once were alienated and hostile in mind, doing evil deeds, Christ has now reconciled in his body of flesh by his death, in order to present you holy and blameless and above reproach before him" (Cl 1:21, ESV).

CHRIST is PRE-EMINENT OVER ALL DAYS

As we have seen, the two great gifts of Christ are *life* and a *future*, which then place upon us the duty of finding and doing God's will, so that we shall receive heaven's prize. Can there be a higher joy, a more satisfying life than this? See how it changes the dismal sense of *"a hundred years from now"*! –

> It will all be the same in a hundred years –
> What a spell-word to conjure up smiles and tears!
> . . .
> For the rust that consumeth the sword of the brave,
> Eats, too, at the chain of the manacled slave,
> And the conqueror's frowns and his victim's tears
> Will all be the same in a hundred years.
> . . .
> For Time, as he speeds on invisible wings,
> Disenamels and withers earth's costliest things,
> And the knight's white plume, and the shepherd's crook,
> And the minstrel's pipe, and the scholar's book,
> And the emperor's crown, and his Cossack's spears,
> Will be dust alike in a hundred years!
>
> Then what meaneth the chase after phantom joys,
> And the breaking of human hearts for toys,
> And the veteran's pride in his crafty schemes,

And the passions of youth for its darling dreams,
And the aiming at ends we can never span,
And the deadly aversions of man for man?
To what end is this conflict of hopes and fears?
If 'tis all the same in a hundred years?

Ah, 'tis not the same in a hundred years,
How clear soever that motto appears;
For know ye not that beyond the grave,
Far, far beyond where the cedars wave
On the Syrian mountains, and where the stars
Come glittering forth in their golden cars,
There bloometh a land of perennial bliss,
Where we smile to think of the tears in this?
And the pilgrim reaching that radiant shore
Hath the thought of death in his heart no more,
But layeth his staff and sandals down
For the victor's wreath and the Saviour's crown

. . .

Then be glad, my heart, and forget thy tears;
For 'tis NOT the same in a hundred years! [100]

But that confidence in its turn pre-supposes one great fact – that **Christ reigns supreme over time**, and can and does either control or shape every event toward fulfilling the Father's ultimate purpose. Indeed, in our affirmation of Christ, this is the noblest expression of our faith –

> *He is the image of the invisible God, the firstborn of all creation. For by him all things were created, in heaven and on earth, visible and invisible, whether thrones or dominions or rulers or authorities – all things were*

---

[100] Elizabeth Doten (late 19th cent., just over 100 years ago!)

created through him and for him. And he is before all things, and in him all things hold together. And he is the head of the body, the church. He is the beginning, the firstborn from the dead, that in everything he might be preeminent (Cl 1:15-18, ESV).

ALEXANDER AND BUCEPHALUS

Plutarch tells this story about Alexander when he was still the young crown prince of ancient Macedon –

> When a Thessalian horse-trader brought Bucephalus [101] to Philip and offered it to him for the extortionate sum of thirteen talents, the king and his friends proceeded to some level ground to try the horse's paces. They found that he was very savage and unmanageable, for he allowed no one to mount him, and paid no attention to any man's voice, but refused to allow any one to approach him. On this Philip became angry, and bade them take the vicious intractable brute away.
>
> Alexander, who was present, said, "What a fine horse they are ruining because they are too ignorant and cowardly to manage him." Philip at first was silent, but when Alexander repeated this remark several times, and seemed greatly distressed, he said, "Do you blame your elders, as if you knew more than they, or were better able to manage a horse?" "This horse, at any

---

[101] The literal meaning of this word is "bull's head." It is conjectured that this refers to the mark with which the horse was branded, not to his appearance.

rate," answered Alexander, "I could manage better than anyone else." "And if you cannot manage him," retorted his father, "what penalty will you pay for your forwardness?" "I will pay," said Alexander, "the price of the horse."

While the others were laughing and settling the terms of the wager, Alexander ran straight up to the horse, took him by the bridle, and turned him to the sun. He had noticed that the horse's shadow dancing before his eyes alarmed him and made him restive. He then spoke gently to Bucephalus, and patted him on the back with his hand, until he perceived that he no longer snorted so wildly. Then, dropping his cloak, he lightly leaped upon his back. He now steadily reined him in, without violence or blows, and as he saw that the horse was no longer ill-tempered, but only eager to gallop, he let him go, boldly urging him to full speed with his voice and heel.

Philip and his friends were at first silent with terror; but when he wheeled the horse round, and rode up to them exulting in his success, they burst into a loud shout. It is said that his father wept for joy, and, when he dismounted, kissed him, saying, "My son, seek for a kingdom worthy of yourself – for Macedonia is too small for you!" ([102])

([102]) <u>Lives of the Noble Grecians and Romans</u>, by Plutarch (c. 46-120); tr. by A. H. Clough, with some amendments. From a now lost source, I gathered the following continuation of the story – "But – continued on next page

That is how we should feel about this world and all its earthly splendour. It is too small for us. We are destined in Christ for higher and greater things, for we are indeed co-heirs with Christ of all the majesty of heaven. Never lose your grip on that glorious prize!

---

even the ambitious Crown Prince Alexander of Macedon might have hesitated to predict for himself the triumphs that were to come. In the 20 years remaining to him, he was to overthrow the great empire of Persia and create another realm, greater by far, stretching from the Balkans to India. Born to be king of Macedon, a small, mountainous kingdom near Greece, he made himself the emperor of Egypt and western Asia by the age of 26. The boy and the horse were not to part for many years. The Roman historian Curtius wrote that Bucephalus always lowered its head to help Alexander mount him, and Arrian, a Greek general in the service of Rome, writing in the 2nd century A.D., noted that the horse never again allowed anyone but Alexander to ride it. The two became a famous pair. Bucephalus remained capable of great speed for the 17 years during which they were together. When the great horse died in 326 B.C., Alexander built a city, Bucephala, over its grave (on the west bank of the Hydaspes river, possibly the city now known as Jhelum in Pakistan).

Chapter Eleven

THE TRANSFORMING CHRIST

> I wish that there were some wonderful place
> Called the Land of Beginning Again,
> Where all our mistakes
> And all our heartaches,
> And all of our poor selfish grief,
> Could be dropped like a shabby coat at the door
> And never put on again!
> – Anonymous

Do not lie to one another. Have you not put off your old self, with all its habits? Have you not put on your new self, which, as you grow in knowledge, is being renewed in the image of its Creator? So then, clothe yourselves with the kind of garments that belong to God's chosen and beloved people, full of compassion, generosity, gentleness, and patience. (Cl 3:9-10, 12)

This *"putting-off"* and *"putting-on"* is one of the most radical and extraordinary ideas in the entire Bible! Virtually all Christian doctrines have some kind of parallel in other sacred writings. But not this, for nothing like it has ever been found in any pre-Christian literature. It stands unique in scripture – startling, provoking, and revealing a breathtaking life-potential that had never before entered human thought. [103]

Paul talks about us Christians, and the two parts of our human nature – the "***old self***" and the "***new self***", or what KJV calls "the old man" in Adam and "the new man" in Christ. He says that in Christ we should "***put off***" the old and "***put on***" the new. And with this arresting and innovative revelation, he solves an ancient dilemma – "How can I escape what I <u>am</u> and become what I should <u>be</u>?" Paul says that the answer lies in learning how to "clothe" ourselves with Christ, by coming into an ever-deeper faith union with him. This indeed is the place yearned for by the poet, a *Land of Beginning Again*, where we can shed our darker self like an old "shabby coat at the door", and enter into a wonderful new world of victory and wholeness in Christ! Everyone who truly discovers Christ and comes into full union with him soon finds that

> Heaven above is softer blue,
> And earth around is sweeter green;
> Something lives in every hue,
> That Christless eyes have never seen.
> Birds with softer songs o'erflow,
> And the flowers with deeper beauty shine,
> Since I know, as now I know,
> I am his and he is mine! [104]

---

[103] There are however, hints of it in earlier Hebrew writings, such as Baruch 5:1-2, "Take off the garment of your sorrow and affliction, O Jerusalem, and put on forever the beauty of the glory from God. Put on the robe of the righteousness from God; put on your head the diadem of the glory of the Everlasting." The idea is not the same as Paul's, but it may well have helped to spark Paul's revelation.

Paul says that the first step we need to take to enter this new realm is to deal with –

THE OLD SELF

The ancient Romans looked upon the murder of a parent by a child with particular loathing. They saw parricide as an attack on the basic foundation of society and thus on society itself. To the Romans it was a crime akin to treason, not only against the sacred family unit, but also against the state, and against the natural order of the world. For such a crime they reserved the most severe penalties. According to the Roman historian Suetonius, a parricide was executed by first being cruelly beaten and then sewn into a sack, along with a live dog, a rooster, a viper, and an ape – animals that represented the four different vices that had led to the awful crime. [105] So the criminal perished most miserably.

We are like that wretched parricide. Sewn into the sack of our own fallen condition. We find ourselves burdened with what the apostle calls *"the old self"* – that is, our fallen human nature, enmeshed in a body of sin, utterly without hope of escape except for the salvation offered by Christ.

These works of the "old self" hang around our neck like the rotting corpse of their victim that people guilty of infanticide

---

[104] From the hymn Loved with Everlasting Love, by G. Wade Robinson.

[105] De Vita Caesarum, Augustus, Sec. 18.

were long ago condemned to carry. (106) Paul summarises them as –

- **five _sexual_ sins** – going (as I read somewhere) from the outer _act_ to the inner _motivation_ (Cl 3:5, in the words of the NRSV) –
    - fornication
    - impurity
    - passion
    - evil desire
    - covetousness, which is idolatry.

- **five _verbal_ sins** – but this time going from the inner _motivation_ to the outer _act_ (vs. 8,9) –
    - anger
    - wrath
    - malice
    - slander
    - foul talk

We are all included in those lists! The "old self" is a perpetual problem, especially for someone who is hindered by it from reflecting both the outer behaviour and the inner beauty of Christ. Indeed, everyone should desire to be rid of the works of the "old self" and to walk fully in the triumph and abundance of Christ. Why? –

---

(106) Cp. 1 Mc 1:60-61, which suggests that the mothers were executed by hanging their murdered babies from their necks; but see also 2 Mc 6:10 and Josephus Antiquities Bk 12, Ch 5:4.

BECAUSE THE WRATH OF GOD IS UPON THEM.

"It is because of such conduct that God will fall in anger upon people who continue to disobey him" (Cl 3:6).

Perhaps strangely, people hardly need to be told about the wrath to come. From earliest times men and women, both godly and ungodly alike, have had a deep inner sense that in the end they cannot avoid being punished for their sin. For example, the Roman philosopher Seneca (who was a contemporary of Paul, although of course they were quite unaware of each other's existence) wrote –

> Again, let us suppose the good gods choose
> To hide forbidden love; let us suppose
> They lend to lawless intercourse protection
> Denied to greater crimes – think of the price,
> The penalty within, the conscious heart's
> Deep dread, the mind burdened with guilt, the soul
> That dare not face itself. Some may have sinned
> With safety, none with conscience unimpaired. [107]

The noble Roman, who was a friend of Caesar, understood well that no sin goes unnoticed, nor unpunished. And again –

> ... even the most depraved characters retain some sense of good, are not blind to their own depravity but prefer to ignore it ... (So) concealment is little comfort to the sinner, because though concealment may be his luck, it cannot restore his confidence. True enough –

---

[107] <u>Four Tragedies and Octavia</u>; *Phaedra* - Act One. Tr. EF Watling; Penguin Books, London, 1970; pg. 104-105.

> crime can be kept hidden, but it cannot be enjoyed without fear. ... (The) chief and greatest punishment that sinners suffer is the fact they have sinned; no crime ... can remain unpunished, because crime is its own punishment. [108]

BECAUSE THE PEOPLE OF GOD MUST LOATHE ALL THAT IS UNGODLY

> *"If you truly have been raised up with Christ, then you should seek those things that are above, where Christ is, enthroned at the right hand of God!" (vs. 1).*

Make no mistake, there is no victory without this. Like Jesus himself, we must learn to *"love righteousness and hate iniquity"* (He 1:9). And it is against that background of hating all that belongs to the old fallen self, and yearning to be clothed with the unsullied holiness of Christ that Paul tells us to put off the "old self" and to put on

THE NEW SELF

Paul's method is *faith*, which is based upon a revelation of what God has done for us in Christ. Search and see – you will find no reference to tears, pleadings, bitter struggle, and the like! The process is not one of *will-power* against *sin-power*; nor of physical energy against spiritual weakness; but of *"faith"* against what Paul calls the *"flesh"*.

We may ask two vital questions –

---

[108] *Epistulae Morales* #97; ibid; pg.317.

WHAT DOES FAITH DO?

In his *History*, the Greek writer Herodotus (*circa* BC 484-425) tells the story of how news was secretly sent from Susa (in Persia) to Sparta, revealing that the Persian emperor Xerxes was about to launch an attack upon Greece –

> The Spartans had been informed before anyone else in Greece that King Xerxes was preparing an expedition against Hellas. ... And they got this information in a strange manner; for Demaratos [109] ... being in Susa and having been informed of the coming invasion, determined to send a warning to the Spartans. Now in no other way was he able to signify it, for there was danger that should he be discovered he would be severely punished. But he contrived thus – he took a folding tablet, scraped off the wax that was upon it, and then scratched his warning directly upon the wood of the tablet. Having done so he then melted the wax and poured it over the writing, so that the tablet (being carried without writing upon it) might not provoke any trouble from the guards who patrolled the road. Then when it had arrived at Lacedemon, the Lacedemonians were not able to make conjecture of the matter; until at last, as I am informed, Gorgo, the daughter of Cleomenes and wife of Leonidas, suggested a plan of which she had herself

---

[109] A former king of Sparta who had been dethroned and sent into exile. He fled to Persia, befriended King Darius, and later accompanied Xerxes in his wars. He was given several Persian cities to govern, and died while still in exile.

thought. She bade them scrape the wax and they would find writing upon the wood; and doing as she said they found the writing and read it, and after that they sent notice to the other Hellenes. [110]

So the Greeks were warned and were able to make preparations in good time to thwart the Persian invasion.

There is a sense in which the promises of God in scripture are like that hidden message. Although they are written clearly on the printed page, somehow they sit there lifeless until faith scours off the surface and penetrates to the inner heart of the revelation of God.

Isaiah hints at this –

> *I will give you treasures from dark caverns, and riches from secret places, so that you will know that I am the Lord (45:3).*

Seldom do gold nuggets and shimmering emeralds lie on the surface. The earth usually demands much patient and persevering toil before it will surrender its jewels to the miner. So it is with scripture. While sometimes a gem of promise may leap off the page and catch us unawares, or we may sometimes stumble inadvertently upon some sweet word of grace, mostly the Bible yields its most sparkling prizes only to those who labour long in reading, meditation, and prayer.

Or to change the analogy – when we read the promise there often seems to be a hiatus, a deep and wide chasm, between where we are and where the promise stands. There is a sense

---

[110] From <u>The History of Herodotus</u>, based on Macauley's translation; Bk 7, Ch. 238.

of unreality about the promise, as if it were artificial, lacking pulsating life.

How can that gap be bridged? How can my heart and the promise be brought together? How can splatters of ink on paper suddenly begin to surge with limitless energy and irresistible strength? How can mere words assume the immeasurable power of God?

Only by a revelation of the word that comes from believing prayer. Those two (faith and prayer) mingled together with the promise of God transform each promise into the flashing sword of the Holy Spirit, able to cut down all the works of the enemy and to enliven us with all the resources of heaven.

Paul understood the huge importance of this principle –

> *I never stop giving thanks for you, as I remember you in my prayers, praying that the God of our Lord Jesus Christ, the Father of glory, will give you a spirit of wisdom and of **revelation** in your knowledge of him, having the eyes of your hearts **enlightened**, so that you may **know** what is the hope to which he has called you, what are the riches of his glorious inheritance in the saints, and how immeasurably great is his power **at work in us who believe**! (Ep 1:16-19; and see also Cl 1:9-10)*

So follow the apostle's example, and never stop praying until your spiritual eyes have indeed been opened, and a revelation of the promise of God sparkles into explosive life in your soul. Then, sensing, near at hand *"the immeasurable greatness of his power"* you can begin to *"put off"* the old, and *"put on"* the new!

The metaphor is one of putting off old rags and putting on new garments (the Greek words in vs. 8-10 have that particular meaning). Faith scornfully dismisses the one, and eagerly embraces the other.

HOW DOES FAITH DO THIS?

FAITH REMEMBERS

During the Feudal period of European history the households of princes and high-ranking noblemen included a ***whipping-boy***. He was usually of the same age as the heir of the house, but of lower rank, and was raised with him, and generally treated as an equal. But if the young prince or noblemen misbehaved, or grew lazy in his schoolwork, and his father, who would normally administer punishment, was away, then the whipping boy was flogged instead. It was unthinkable that anyone of lower rank than the noble child should be allowed to beat him. But any high official could whip the surrogate boy. [111]

Since the two boys were playmates, in most cases the prince would be ashamed to become the cause of his friend's pain and so would behave himself. But not always. In any case, once the other boy had been lashed, it is unlikely that the guilt-stricken prince would then demand that he too should

---

[111] According to Brewster, "Barnaby Fitzpatrick so stood for Edward VI, and Mungo Murray for Charles I. When Henry IV of France abjured Protestantism and was received into the Catholic Church in 1593, Bishop Duperron and Cardinal d'Ossat were sent to Rome to obtain the king's absolution. They knelt in the portico of St Peter's singing the Miserere. At each verse a blow with a switch was dealt to their shoulders." (Dictionary of Phrase and Fable in loc.) Mark Twain, in The Prince and the Pauper (1882), portrayed Tom Canty as whipping boy for Prince Edward, the son of Henry VIII (Chapter 15). Several web sites contain the full text of this book.

feel the whip's awful bite. Nor could he do so even if he did wish it, for the law forbade any lesser person to strike him.

Faith remembers that this is what Christ has endured for us. He was our Surrogate. He suffered in our stead. He bore the punishment that was rightly ours. Yet his rank is as far above sinners as heaven is above earth. Nor were our faults mere childish pranks, juvenile malfeasance. Rather they were, and are, offences against the highest glory of God, deserving death. But he, the Author of all Life, yielded himself to death in our place.

But we are often stricken with shame at the thought of the Innocent dying for the guilty. We feel it is only right that we too should suffer. We want to add our own anguish to that of Christ. Surely his death, by itself alone, cannot entirely be adequate to atone for all our wrongdoing and make peace with God?

But remember the prince and the whipping boy. No matter how much the noble lad shrank in shame from the cries of his playmate, nor how fervently he wished to assuage his guilt by sharing in the other's pain, he could do nothing but freely accept what was offered, and escape without even a gentle slap.

Let us then cease from our own works altogether, and find complete safety and satisfaction in Christ, in whom we have been made the very righteousness of God himself. Why cling to the tattered rags of your own good works, when the splendour of heaven's holiness is offered free of all charge to all who simply believe?

FAITH RENOUNCES

The rule that we must hate iniquity and love righteousness was recognised long before Jesus espoused it –

> It is for you to avoid doing what God hates. Do not say, "It was he who led me astray," for he has no use for sinful men. The Lord hates every kind of vice; you cannot love it and still fear him. When he made man in the beginning, he left him free to take his own decisions; if you choose, you can keep the commandments; whether or not you keep faith is yours to decide. He has set before you fire and water; reach out and take which you choose; before man lie life and death, and whichever he prefers is his. ... Turn to the Lord and have done with sin; make your prayer in his presence, and so lessen your offence. Come back to the Most High, renounce wrongdoing, and hate intensely what he abhors. [112]

Yet that still seems to leave us with the same problem – even when I do "renounce wrongdoing and hate intensely what God abhors", and even when I love righteousness with a passion, the "old self" keeps on intruding its ugliness. How then can I truly "have done with sin"? How can I rid myself of all that belongs to my fallen nature?

Paul's remedy is simply *"put the works of the old self to death"* (Cl 3:5).

But how can we do that?

Shall we emulate the flagellants across the ages who have struggled to kill the *"flesh"* by severe fasting and self-imposed pain? Shall we, as they did, begin whipping

---

[112] <u>The Wisdom of Sirach</u> (15:11-17; 17:25-26, NEB). Sirach was a rabbi who flourished in the late 3rd century B.C. His writings were translated into Greek by his grandson, circa 180-175 B.C.

ourselves, denying ourselves all pleasure, and inflicting upon ourselves all manner of misery? Can we gain merit with God only by violently subduing our bodies, by torturing and mutilating ourselves, or by similar harsh means?

Yet who has ever succeeded in that endeavour?

Neither the most appalling savagery nor the most pitiless anguish ever advanced the flagellants of old so much as the breadth of one hair nearer to God. [113] No, the simple fact is this – if we cannot approach the throne by virtue of faith alone, then we shall never be able to do so. No quantity of prayer, fasting, sacrifice, toil, struggle, tears, torment, nor anything else we could ever imagine or do will earn us the right to take even one step toward the Throne of Heaven. If we cannot boldly draw near by the blood of the everlasting covenant, then we are banished for ever. But let us not despair! On the contrary –

> **_Let us boldly enter the Holiest by the blood of Jesus_**, *by the new and living way that he inaugurated for us, through the veil, that is, his body. Yes, since we now have a High Priest over the house of God,* **_let us approach God with a true heart in full assurance of faith_** *(He 10:19-22).*

And again –

> *God has an eternal purpose, which he has accomplished through Christ Jesus our Lord, in whom, through our faith in him,* **_we may now boldly approach God with all confidence_** *(Ep 3:11-12).*

---

[113] See *Addendum* 10, The Saints of Old.

Mark this deeply – for every true Christian ultimate capitulation to sin must be impossible. Then mark it again – you do not have to accept your weakness – you need not stay the same – you can be different!

FAITH RESTS

Note Paul's amazing boldness: *"Have you not (already) put off your old self? Have you not (already) put on your new self?"*

As far as God is concerned, the work is already done in the heavenlies, but we must implement it in daily life; hence he says *"put off all these things . . . "* (vs. 8, in which he uses the same verb as Luke uses in *Acts 7:58* – *"The witnesses took off their coats..."*).

Here then is where faith is bold. Despite appearances it affirms the impossible. It declares true what God has spoken, and everything else a lie. It shows dauntless courage, and extraordinary daring in grasping all that the Lord is offering.

Herodotus tells a fascinating story that well illustrates the kind of heart we should have in response to the riches the Father has laid before us in Christ –

> Now the family of Alcmaion was distinguished in Athens in the earliest times also, and from the time of Alcmaion ... they became very greatly distinguished. ,,, For King Crœsus of Lydia, having heard .. that (Alcmaion) had done him a great service, sent for him to Sardis; and when he came, he offered to give him a gift of as much gold as he could carry away at once upon his own person. With a view to this gift, its nature being such, Alcmaion made preparations and used appliances as follows – he put on a large tunic leaving a deep fold in the tunic to hang down in front, and he

drew on his feet the widest boots which he could find, and so went to the treasury to which they conducted him. Then he fell upon a heap of gold-dust, and first he packed in by the side of his legs so much of the gold as his boots would contain, and then he filled the whole fold of the tunic with the gold and sprinkled some of the gold dust on the hair of his head and took some into his mouth, and having so done he came forth out of the treasury, with difficulty dragging along his boots and resembling anything in the world rather than a man; for his mouth was stuffed full, and every part of him was swelled out: and upon Crœsus came laughter when he saw him, and he not only gave him all that, but also presented him in addition with more not inferior in value to that. Thus this house became exceedingly wealthy, and thus the Alcmaion of whom I speak became a breeder of chariot-horses and won a victory at Olympia. [114]

How often the Lord must yearn for the same kind of boldness from his children. So often we treat the Almighty as if he were as parsimonious or as poor as we are. But I have learned this over the years: you cannot anger God by asking him for too much; but you will certainly aggravate him if you ask for too little!

The treasure-house of heaven lies before you, with the door wide open. The righteousness of the Lord himself lies there in overflowing heaps, and victory over all the deprivations of Satan is piled up, and cascades of pardon, grace, peace, joy,

---

[114] Op. Cit. Bk. VI, Sec. 125.

holiness, along with weapons of war that guarantee a triumphant entrance into heaven's golden portals on that great coming day!

FAITH REJOICES

All that belongs to the nature of Christ is already mine (Cl 3:12-14). Thus, I am not struggling to be kind, I *am* kind! I am not struggling for holiness, since through union with Christ by faith I *am* holy. All that is in Christ is in me in Christ, the hope of glory (Cl 1:27).

Yet, though he says that we have already *"put off the old and put on the new"*, still he tells us to do so! – see vs. 12; and cp. *Ephesians 4:22-24.*

Here we confront one of the constant principles of scripture: what God has done for us potentially in Christ, we must seize and bring into reality by faith.

The more firmly you declare by faith the truth of what God says about you in Christ, the more firmly will the character of Christ be displayed in your life. So set yourself to speak the desired result, not what your natural eye sees. *Faith* is the way to victory, not many tears and prayers – by *faith* release all that Christ is and *all* that you are in Christ! For indeed

> *it is nothing to be either a Greek or a Jew, to observe some religious ritual or not to observe it, to be civilised or uncivilised, a free person or a slave. Only Christ matters. He alone is all and he is in us all! (Cl 3:11)*

And we who believe are every one of us complete in him!

Chapter Twelve

THE GREATEST THING IN THE WORLD

> *I am willing to toss everything into the rubbish dump, if only I may know Christ, and the power of his resurrection, and the prize of the upward call of God (Ph3:8,10,14).*

At first sight, that seems to be a piece of wild hyperbole. Does he truly mean *everything*? Wife, children, house, car, all worldly possessions, the whole earth, the sun, moon, stars, the entire universe? Well that depends upon what one hopes to gain. The question really asks – *is there something so valuable that to gain it would be worth paying any price you could imagine?*

Yes, there is. In fact, Paul had in mind three great treasures that surpass the combined wealth of the entire creation –

THE GREATEST PERSON YOU CAN KNOW

> *I will pay any price, if only I can know Christ.*

Rudyard Kipling once wrote a poem around the idea, "He travels the fastest, who travels alone" –

> One may fall, but he falls by himself –
>   Falls by himself, with himself to blame.
> One may attain, and to him is the pelf,
>   Loot of the city in Gold or Fame.

> Plunder of earth shall be all his own
> Who travels the fastest and travels alone.
>
> – 3rd Stanza, "The Witness"

But what a dreary prospect – rich, yet *alone*! Paul recognises rather that the greatest happiness is to have a true companion. The wise man had the same idea, when he said that to be married to a good woman was to have wealth *"far above rubies"*.

But the corollary is that loneliness must be the greatest misery. Can you imagine any greater nightmare than to be marooned on a barren island, condemned to live and die there, utterly alone, perhaps for many years before death ends the aching misery.

Yet we are all like that desolate mariner; we are a people marooned on the desert shores of life. Carole Simcox expressed this, when she described our condition in the neologism, "solitariness" – [115]

> Solitariness is not solitude, nor privacy. nor loneliness, nor spiritual solipsism,[116] nor even aloneness. People experience solitariness when the chilling, scary, desolating truth bursts upon

---

[115] Christian Century; Apr 18, 1984; pg. 398.

[116] Solipsism comes from two Latin words, which taken together mean "alone with oneself". The term is used to describe a school of philosophy that argues that I have no sure ground upon which to believe in the existence of anything except my own mind. The idea is similar to the one expressed by Descartes (who, however, was not a solipsist) in his famous formula – "Cogito, ergo sum" – "I think, therefore I am." Solipsism presses the idea to its limit, and concludes, "I alone exist." That is, since I can prove the existence of nothing else, I must assert that there is no reality outside of my own mind. Solipsism is, of course, absurd.

them that they are not like anybody else. It is an acute, and for most of us, unpleasant sense of our uniqueness, our differentness from all other human beings ... To whom can I bear my soul, showing myself as I really am? Who can possibly understand me if he or she has never walked in my moccasins? . . .

And all those fellow human beings around me are, must be, as different from me as I am from them. Solitariness is the doom of each.

Thus also Edgar Allen Poe once wrote –

All that we see or seem is but a dream within a dream. [117]

– and somewhere, Charles Dickens wrote –

Here is a wonderful fact to reflect upon, that every human creature is constituted to be that profound secret and mystery to every other.

– likewise, Blaise Pascal –

The eternal silence of these infinite spaces frightens me ... When I consider the short duration of my life, swallowed up in the eternity before and after, the little space that I fill, or can even see, engulfed in the infinite immensity of spaces of which I am ignorant, and which know me not, I am frightened! [118]

But Solomon said it earlier –

---

[117] Poem (1849), *A Dream Within a Dream*; line 10.
[118] <u>Pensees</u> # 206, 205.

> *The heart alone knows its own bitterness, nor can any stranger share its joy (Pr 14:10)*

So we find that we are separated from each other by a hiatus that not even the deepest love or friendship can wholly bridge.

At the time of this writing my wife and I have been most happily married for 60 years. I suppose that we know each other as deeply, as warmly, as delightfully as any two people on this troubled planet can ever hope to achieve. Yet in the end we plumb each other only in the shallows not the depths of life. My wife understands me well, yet she perceives only a small part of what travels through my mind, my heart, my spirit each day. I dare not disclose all to her. Indeed, I could not do so even if I wished to, because much that lies within me defies expression by mere words. In the end we are strangers to each other, just as we are to all those around us. We must each ultimately walk alone.

Why is this? The cause is sin, which breaks the bonds within ourselves, and with our neighbours, and with God. This indeed is the state of all unbelievers; it is the ultimate hell, when sin has its full sway, and every doomed soul will be alone, *alone for ever!* It makes a mockery of the inebriate's claim that if he is sent to hell, at least he will be with his drinking mates. Ah! but not so, for the entire population of hell is precisely ... *one* soul – for that is how it will seem to each isolated person incarcerated in that place of *"outer darkness"* (cp. Mt 8:12; 22:13; 25:30).

<u>But Christ is the great Mender</u> (Ep 2:13-14). Through knowing him, we begin to know ourselves, our neighbour, and our God. For us Christians this process has begun now, and will reach its consummation in the resurrection. Then what infinite delight! What measureless joy! What surpassing fellowship and unbounded love! To know Christ as I am known by him (1 Co 13:12), and through Christ to know fully and to be fully known by all who will share paradise with me – ah! there is bliss beyond measure!

To gain this knowledge, said Paul, is worth any cost! And indeed it *will* cost me everything, yet also cost me nothing! It will cost me *nothing*, because scripture itself bids me to come boldly and to drink freely of the water of life in Christ. It will also cost me *everything*, for as Jesus said,

> *If any of you come to me yet remain unwilling to abandon your father, mother, wife, children, brothers, and sisters, as well as your own life, you cannot be my disciple. And if you refuse to pick up your cross and follow me then you cannot be my disciple. (Lu 14:26-27)*

If all real happiness comes from having a true friend, then the greatest of all happiness must come from fellowship with the greatest of all Friends, the greatest Person you can know, *Jesus!*

THE GREATEST POWER YOU CAN EXPERIENCE

> *I will pay any price, if only I can know the power of his resurrection.*

When I was a boy, perhaps 9 years old, I was given a Bible that was well-illustrated by copies of great works of art, inserted between its pages. Only one of those paintings made a lasting impression on me. It was a picture by the French artist Jean-Léon Gérôme (1824-1904) entitled *The Last Prayer*. The scene is the great Colosseum in Rome. Thousands of screaming spectators pack the tiered seats. Around the perimeter of the arena many crosses have been planted, each bearing a tortured Christian martyr who is not only nailed to its beam but also is being burnt to death. At one side some lions are emerging from their cages, ready to fall upon a huddle of people who are kneeling in the middle of the sandy expanse. They comprise a small congregation of perhaps thirty men, women, young people, and children. Their elderly pastor stands in their midst, head raised heavenward, leading his people in prayer. Together they are calmly awaiting a hideous death – torn to pieces by the starving animals.

For a child, it was a dramatic and terrifying picture. Yet I often turned to it, and gazed upon it with a kind of fascinated horror.

But what most appalled me was not the flames consuming the crucified victims, nor the fierce lions who with implacable indifference to human anguish were about to tear apart their living prey, nor even the blood-crazed shrieks of the watching crowd. Awful as those things were, I was upset most by the presence of at least one child my own age in the kneeling and praying group. I could not understand how any loving parent, or true pastor, or friend, could condemn a little boy to such an unspeakable death, nor how the child could kneel there so serenely, his hands joined in prayer, waiting for the lion's jaw to clamp upon his neck. Although it was only a painting, and in a sense fictitious, yet I knew that it portrayed events that had often happened, [119] and I wondered why those women and children were not cursing

---

[119] However, while Christians were certainly burnt to death and thrown to the lions by the Roman authorities, there is some doubt about whether or not any of them were put to death in the Colosseum – "The tradition that Christians were martyred there remains a possibility but has no ancient basis, dating from Benedict XIV's consecration of the structure to the martyrs in 1750." (The New International Dictionary of the Christian Church, ed. JD Douglas; Zondervan Corporation, Grand Rapids, Michigan, 1974; pg. 241.

the men who had brought them so deliberately to such unutterable misery? Quite the contrary, they all, both young and old, seemed content to die. They were like the 17-year old Origen, whose father was martyred in the persecution of Septimus Severus in 202. Origen was so eager to join with his father in martyrdom that his mother had to hide his clothes while he was bathing. This was enough to prevent him from rushing off to the place of execution and declaring himself also to be a Christian! [120]

How can such zeal be explained. Were they all simply crazed religious fanatics? Or was there a far more powerful force at work?

The answer – after centuries of bleak despair in the presence of death, the church was now certain that Christ had for ever conquered that hideous enemy! The martyrs had felt the power of Christ's resurrection so strongly that all fear of death was banished. They knew deep within themselves that Christ was both with them and in them, the hope of glory (Cl 1:27), and they could sing their way through the most unspeakable torments into paradise and the promised golden crown (2 Ti 4:8; Ja 1:12; 1 Pe 5:4).

But in the larger world, death was still a thing of horror. Indeed, it is difficult for us to imagine how profoundly the ancients feared death, and how limitless was their horror

---

[120] She knew that he would be far more horrified by running naked through the city than by burning at the stake! Five decades later he gained his wish. He suffered brutal torture during the Decian persecution in 250, and, although he was released from prison still refusing to deny Christ, he never recovered his health and died some three years later. You will find the full story of Origen (including his self-castration) in any comprehensive book on church history.

and despair in its presence. But suppose you had been brought up to believe that the only destination you could hope for after death was to be admitted to Hades, the hideous realm of its eponymous god. Hades was portrayed as an enormous cavern, deep in the bowels of the planet, presided over by a deity so terrifying that the Greeks were reluctant to pronounce his name, and instead called him Pluto (from a Greek word meaning riches, because his domain embraced all the treasures of gold, silver, and precious stones that are hidden in the earth).

The myth said that when a person's body died, his spirit, or shade, using a coin that had been placed by the mourners in the mouth of the dead body, first had to bribe the boatman Charon to carry it across the dark river Styx,. But as soon as the shade disembarked from the ferry, it was met by Cerberus, a monstrous snarling dog with three heads, a serpent for a tail, and serpents wrapped around its neck. If the shade managed to escape the dog's slavering jaws, it faced at once a new terror, the Furies. These were gruesome female sub-deities who had heads like dogs, snake-entwined hair, pitch-black bodies, awful blood-dripping eyes, and who carried brass-studded thongs to scourge the guilty dead onward and through the ghastly gates of Hades. Once those pitiless gates had closed behind a shade, the Greeks believed that not even mighty Zeus, supreme ruler over the gods, could rescue the unhappy captive from the relentless hands of Pluto and his horde of wrathful guards.

When such ideas were the only ones people had heard from infancy, it is hardly surprising that death was faced with measureless despair. For example, here are three poems I have selected from many similar ones in *The Greek Anthology* – [121]

> My daughter's dear child here I hold on my lap; so
> I used to hold him of old in those days
> When with living eyes we both looked on the sun:
> Now that he's dead, I still hold him – for I
> Am dead too. *(#46)*

***

> Throwing her arms around her father,
> her eyes streaming with pale tears,
> Erato spoke these last words:
> "Oh father, I am leaving you; over my eyes
> Death draws his darkness –
> and I go into the dark." *(#103)*

***

> Aristocrateia,
> You've crossed the dark stream
> Young and unwed, alas !
> Your mother's left with just
> The tears she sheds, when
> Often now she weeping lies
> Prostrate upon your tomb. *(#201)*

Many other grief-drenched verses are scattered through the *Anthology*. The ancients could find no comfort, no hope, no promise anywhere in the myths they had long believed about life after death. Only a despairing nightmare existed, of cold, bleak Hades, ruled by Pluto and his awful Furies, and the revulsion of a dark, cheerless eternity.

Into that scene the gospel came with a happy cry of triumph over death, gained by the resurrection of Christ. And about

---

[121] Ed. Peter Jay; Penguin Books Ltd., 1986.

his resurrection the Christians had no doubt; rather, they rejoiced with Luke that after his death and burial, Jesus had shown himself alive by *"many infallible proofs"* (Ac 1:3, KJV).

That certainty banished from them all fear of death, no matter how dire the form it took. They knew two things about the resurrection of Christ –

THE FACT

See Acts 1:3. Several years ago, after Professor Barbara Thiering had presented the "swoon theory"[122] on an Australian TV show, this fine piece of sarcasm appeared in the "Letters" section of *The Sydney Morning Herald* –

> I like Dr Thiering's hypothesis concerning Jesus. Flogged half to death, crucified, then poisoned by a sympathetic Roman guard, Jesus comes to in a cold tomb. Recovering his strength, he rolls back a huge rock, fights off the armed Roman guards, and escapes stark naked into the bush. He then steps into modest retirement in spite of his huge PR coup – classy theory, that.[123]

The reality is that hardly any event from the ancient past has more credibility than the life, death, and resurrection of Jesus of Nazareth. People doubt his resurrection, not because sufficient proof is lacking, but because they dislike the consequences of being obliged to acknowledge that Jesus

---

[122] That is, that Christ did not actually rise from the dead, but rather was resuscitated from a comatose state, lived for many more years, then died naturally, and is still dead.

[123] James McCrudden, Nowra.

is Lord of life and death. For my part, the evidence is overwhelming, and I echo Paul's splendid cry –

> *I am willing to lose everything, and account the whole world a pile of offal, if only I might know Christ and the power of his resurrection, so that I too might be sure of rising from the dead! (Ph 3:8-11)*

THE POWER

See Romans 8:2. The key to the same discovery as the early church made is this – **commitment**. That is, you would rather lose all earth's treasures than *not* know this power. In any case, you will certainly lose them all if you *don't* know it! For if Christ has not conquered death then neither shall we. If Jesus yet lies in the grave, and will be there for ever, then so shall we. But if he lives then we have his personal promise that we who believe in him cannot die either, for death will not be able to hold us. For we who believe, the power of an endless life in Christ is already at work in us! (Jn 11:25-26; 14:19).

THE GREATEST PRIZE YOU CAN GAIN

> *I will pay any price, if only I can gain the prize of the upward call of God.*

The great folly of our time is that people have no vision of the future; they live only for today. Not so Paul. He uses the metaphor of an ancient foot race, with the runners stretching out both arms, straining to win –

Like you, I have not yet won the prize. But there is one thing I can certainly do – forgetting all that is behind me, I will keep on reaching forward to the goal that lies ahead (Ph 3:13).

All Christians should live with such a vision, which is a lesson I learned when, in my mid-teens many years ago, I first read John Bunyan's *Pilgrim's Progress*.

In one place Bunyan tells how some Shepherds escorted the two pilgrims, Christian and Hopeful, to the top of a high hill, from which they could discern the distant glory of the Celestial City, and told them never to lose sight of it –

> By this time the pilgrims had a desire to go forward, and the Shepherds a desire that they should; so they walked together toward the end of the mountains.
>
> Then said the Shepherds one to another, Let us here show the pilgrims the gates of the Celestial City, if they have the skill to look through our perspective-glass. The pilgrims then lovingly accepted the motion – so they had them to the top of a high hill called Clear, and gave them the glass to look . . . (and) they thought they saw something like the gate, and also some of the glory of the place.
>
> (Encouraged by that vision the pilgrims wended their way down the mountain, into the valley below, and continued bravely on their journey, enduring many adventures and overcoming many perils, until they finally gained a splendid welcome into the City of God.)

Do you have that vision ever before *your* eye?

Billy Graham has said that no one is fit to live until they are first ready to die. We might add that no one can truly enjoy the earth until they have first captured the joy of heaven; no one can appreciate the years of time until they have first gripped eternity! This vision makes the cowardly brave, and the weak strong!

CONCLUSION

What happens to the person who makes these discoveries? If you and I are such children of God then we will –

- *never again fear what is happening*, for as the stone was rolled away, so will God fulfil his purpose in us.
- *never again value material things more than spiritual*, for they perish, but we are reaching for the imperishable.
- *never again tolerate sin, nor yield to Satan*, for we are mighty in the resurrection life of Jesus.
- *never again think ourselves unimportant*, for we are children and dear friends of the King.
- *never again undervalue our life*, for Jesus died and rose again and for ever intercedes for us.
- *never again be terrified by death*, for the grave has now between transformed for us into a golden gateway to Paradise!

Addenda

Child Prodigies

Many of the following examples were taken from *The Museum of Conceptual Art* web site; [124] but other sources have also been used. In all these places there are reports of children who displayed extraordinary precocity, which suggests that the precocity of the 12-year old Jesus was not in itself supernatural (Lu 2:42-49). His behaviour was certainly that of a remarkable child, but was not outside the parameters of a proper human nature. It did not mark him as a divine child, possessing attributes that go beyond what any other child could possess. Indeed, many children have shown greater precocity than Jesus displayed.

In making this compilation, I usually ignored reports that appear from time to time in the daily press. The people described in those items are presumably still living, and they may prefer not to have their names mentioned in these pages. Those that I *have* included are here because the relevant information seemed to be more or less in the public domain.

Wikipedia and other online sources contain long lists of child prodigies.

Age One Year

At six months of age, *William J. Sidis Jr.*, the son of a psychiatrist, knew the alphabet.

---

[124] http://museumofconceptualart.com

At the age of 3 months *Jean Louis Cardiac* (born in France in 1719) could repeat the alphabet. At three years old he could read Latin, at four he could translate it into French or English.

Christian Friedrich Heinecken, a German, who was known as the "Infant of Lubeck", from the place where he was born in 1721, is said to have talked within a few hours after his birth. He is known definitely to have been able to speak intelligible German when he was but eight weeks old. Besides his remarkable faculty for numbers, he is said to have known, at the age of one year, all the principal events related in the Pentateuch. At two he was well acquainted with the historical events of the Bible, and at three had a knowledge of universal history, world geography, Latin, and French. People came from all parts to see him, and the Danish king, in order to assure himself of the truth of what he had heard regarding him, had him brought to Copenhagen in 1724. But shortly after this, little Heinecken was taken ill and predicted his own death, which took place in 1725, at the tender age of four. [125]

Age Two Years

By the time he was two, *Ravi Kiran* was able to identify 325 ragas (South Indian melodic scales) and 175 talas (rhythmic cycles). Major newspapers hailed him as an "unprecedented phenomenon", and the Music Academy of Madras awarded him a monthly scholarship.

Miguel Mantilla had the ability to answer such questions as, "In what year will February 4 be a Friday?"

---

[125] Doubts have been expressed about the reliability of these accounts.

Ervin Nyíregyházi (1903-1987) was a Hungarian-born American pianist. His father reported that he had tried to sing before he was 1 year old; that he reproduced tunes correctly before he was 2; that he began to compose at the age of 2; and that he played almost every song he heard correctly on a mouth-organ by the time he reached 3. He played with the Berlin Philharmonic when he was 6. At the age of seven Ervin could identify any note or chord that was played for him. By nine years old, he learned Beethoven sonatas, and at age eleven could play any Bach prelude and fugue from *Book One* of *The Well-Tempered Clavier* transposed into any key. He was known for his musicality just as much as his technique. (Wikipedia).

See also Mohammed Husayn Tabatabai below, under the heading *Age Seven Years*.

Age Three Years

By the time he was three John Stuart Mill, the eminent British social and political thinker, was well into the study of Greek, and by his sixth birthday was familiar with the histories of Xenophon and Herodotus, and the speeches and plays of Lucian.

German mathematician *Carl Friedrich Gauss* taught himself reading and arithmetic before he was three and noticed a calculation mistake in his father's payroll records. He went on to become the greatest mathematician of the 19th century.

JBS Haldane was the son of the renowned scientist JS Haldane. From infancy he was fascinated by his father's work. At age three "he was overheard demanding peevishly of his father, 'But is it oxyhaemoglobin or carboxyhaemoglobin?'" (Bill Bryson, *A Short History of Nearly Everything*, pg. 215)

Wolfgang Amadeus Mozart learned to play the harpsichord at age three and began composing minuets at five years of age. At only four years old he wrote a piano concerto, minuets, and a sonata. His youthful compositions were technically accurate and also difficult to perform, requiring a high level of skill. At seven he composed a full length opera, and at 9 his first symphony.

According to Boswell, at this age <u>Dr Samuel Johnson</u> loved to go to church, and listened avidly to the sermon while perched on his father's shoulder. (*Life of Johnson*, Aetat. 3, 1712.) In the same place Boswell wrote –

> Of the power of his memory, for which he was all his life eminent to a degree almost incredible, the following early instance was told me in his presence at Lichfield, in 1776, by his step-daughter, Mrs. Lucy Porter, as related to her by his mother. When he was a child in petticoats, and had learnt to read, Mrs. Johnson one morning put the common prayer-book into his hands, pointed to the collect for the day, and said, 'Sam, you must get this by heart.' She went up stairs, leaving him to study it – But by the time she had reached the second floor, she heard him following her. 'What's the matter?' said she. 'I can say it,' he replied; and repeated it distinctly, though he could not have read it more than twice.

And again, in *Aetat. 10-16*, [1719-1725], Boswell wrote –

> (Johnson's) school-fellow, Mr. Hector, has obligingly furnished me with many particulars of his boyish days ... He seemed to learn by intuition ... (Indeed) such was the submission and deference with which he was treated, such the desire to obtain his regard, that three of the boys, of whom Mr. Hector was sometimes one, used to come in the morning as his humble

attendants, and carry him to school. One in the middle stooped, while he sat upon his back, and one on each side supported him; and thus he was borne triumphant. Such a proof of the early predominance of intellectual vigor is very remarkable, and does honour to human nature. ...

He discovered a great ambition to excel ... and his memory was so tenacious, that he never forgot anything that he either heard or read. Mr. Hector remembers having recited to him eighteen verses, which, after a little pause, he repeated verbatim, varying only one epithet, by which he improved the line.

Matthew Henry (1662-1714), the renowned Bible commentator, according to his biographer "very early discovered a good mental capacity ... so that he was able to read a chapter from the Bible distinctly when he was but three years old, and was used to make pertinent remarks on what he read."

Age Four Years

At four years old the German composer/conductor *Richard Strauss* could play the piano well, and Spanish composer and piano virtuoso *Albeniz* gave his first public performance.

When he was four, *Jose Raul Casablanca* learned to play chess by watching his father play. When he challenged his father to a game, his father said, "You don't know how to play." Jose replied, "Yes I do," and proceeded to beat his father. He went on to win the world chess championship at age 32.

Tom Wiggins, the blind child of a slave, played the piano as a professional at four. He went on to perform internationally, but away from the piano he could speak only a few words. He died world famous in 1908.

<u>Lucy Hutchinson</u> (born 1620), was the wife of John Hutchinson, who fought for Parliament in the Civil War, and was one of those who signed the death warrant of Charles I. She wrote of herself – "The time of my coming into the world was a considerable mercy to me. It was not in the midnight of popery, nor in the dawn of the gospel's restored day, when light and shades were blended and almost undistinguished, but when the sun of truth was exalted in his progress, and hastening toward a meridian glory. ... By the time I was four years old I could read English perfectly, and having a great memory I was carried to sermons, and while I was very young could remember and repeat them exactly. ... It pleased God that, through the good instructions of my mother, and the sermons she carried me to, I was convinced that the knowledge of God was the most excellent study, and accordingly applied myself to it, and to practise as I was taught." (*The Grand Quarrel*, the Folio Society, London, 1993; pg. 4,5.)

According to John Aubrey (*Brief Lives*), <u>Katherine Philips</u> (1631-64) possessed an astonishing intellectual and spiritual precocity. She had read right through the Bible before she was four, and perhaps had memorised it fully since she could quote copious passages at will. She loved nothing more than going to church and hearing sermons, and before reaching her teens was known to go home after church and write out the entire sermon from memory. Later she gained renown as a poet, and her contemporaries called her the "Matchless Orinda" (a name coined from the classics). She was the first English woman poet to have her work published.

Age Five Years

Once when a second violinist failed to appear for a string quartet performance, the five-year-old *Mozart* took his place, even though he'd never before seen the music.

Ukrainian composer *Sergei Sergeyevich Prokofiev* composed his first piano work.

Spanish pianist *Alicia de Larrocha* gave her first public concert.

By the time she was five, *Gaetana Agnesi* (an 18th century Italian girl) spoke perfect French, and at nine translated from Italian into Latin a discourse on the question of whether or not the education of women should include the humanities (she argued strongly for the affirmative). By her eleventh birthday she could speak fluently in six languages. She was also a genius in mathematics, and developed new mathematical techniques.

At five, pianist *Mieczyslaw Horszowski* played the entire *Bach Inventions* from memory.

Irish mathematician *William Rowan Hamilton* (1805-65) at five years was proficient in Latin, Greek, and Hebrew. By the age of nine he had a knowledge of 13 languages.

Chilian pianist *Claudio Arrau* (1903-91) made his recital debut in Santiago when he was five, with pieces by Mozart, Beethoven and Schumann.

Age Six Years

By the time he was six years old, the great 19th century Russian composer *Tchaikovsky* was not only fluent in reading and speaking his native Russian, but also French and German.

Mozart wrote five short piano pieces when he was six, which are still frequently performed.

There are astonishing cases like *George and Charles*, who were identical twins, and had a phenomenal reputation as human calendar calculators. George at the age of 6 and Charles at the age of 9 could answer spontaneously questions such as, "On what day of the week was your third birthday?" "The year is 31275; on what day of the week will June 6th fall?" Given a date, these twins could swiftly give the day of the week over a span of 80,000 years – 40,000 backward or 40,000 forward (from http://www.gt-cybersource.org.)

Age Seven Years

The British violinist *Yehudi Menuhin* (1916-99), performed as a soloist with the San Francisco Symphony Orchestra when he was seven. Later, when he was still only eleven, the orchestra members wept at the musical skill and insight he displayed in a performance of Beethoven's *Violin Concerto* with the New York Philharmonic.

When he was seven, *Michael Tan* began his studies at Canterbury University for a Bachelor of Science degree in mathematics.

Michael Weinheimer at seven had learned how to calculate square roots. Three years later, he learned how to tie his shoelaces.

In 1999 the *Guardian* contained a report headed "Miracle Child, 7, Memorises Koran". It continued ...

> London – He is little over a metre tall and only seven years old, but each night for the past week crowds of up to 2000 Muslims have been gathering ... to listen in rapt attention to his every word.
>
> *Mohammed Husayn Tabatabai*, from Iran, is being hailed a "miracle child". He has memorised all 600 pages of the Koran ... as

well as hundreds of sayings from the prophet Mohammed.

Last year, aged six, Mohammed became a doctor of religion after proving to Islamic examiners he had grasped the meaning of the verses too.

At the time of this writing a web site devoted to him exists (search for "Tabbatabai") and contains a report of his achievements when he was only *five years* old (in 1997). The writer says –

> The glorious presence of Iran's five-year-old prodigy, Seyyed Mohammad Hossein Tabatabaie at this year's Hajj pilgrimage and his spectacular participation at various Qur'anic events and competitions here, astonished the pilgrims of other countries. His great command over the meaning and the context of the verses surprised the reciters and memorizers of other countries, particularly the Egyptian masters at Mecca's *A Night with the Holy Qur'an* event.
>
> Mohammad Hossein had also separate exclusive meetings with the Saudi Information Minister and the Saudi Minister of Interior in which he answered their questions. When they noticed the precision of Mohammad Hossein's replies regarding the Holy Book and his application of the Holy verses of the Qur'an, they requested him to attend another meeting with the family members of high-ranking Saudi officials to witness his miraculous command over the Holy Qur'an. ... There, Mohammad Hossein for two hours answered numerous questions of a large crowd of Qur'anic masters and reciters, which greatly surprised and

impressed every one. At the end of this meeting, a Saudi Arabian author who has published over a hundred books about the Holy Qur'an so far and trained hundreds of Qur'an reciters himself opined – "Seyyed Mohammad Hossein Tabatabaee is the great miracle of Qur'anic knowledge and the history of Islam has never before witnessed such a prodigy." He further added, "Should I attempt to describe all the various capabilities of Mohammad Hossein to those memorizers of the Holy Qur'an who have not seen him, I'm afraid they may accuse me of in-sincerity, and I won't blame them, because it is truly hard to believe if one has not seen or heard him in person." ...

According to (his father), Mohammad Hossein began memorizing the Qur'an when he was 2.5 years old ... Even when he was a suckling infant, being rocked in his cradle, he heard his mother recite Qur'anic verses. Therefore, one could say, he got acquainted with the Qur'an ever since he was very little and in fact from the very beginning of his life.

When asked, "How good Mohammad Hossein's command is in memorizing the Holy Qur'an!" His father replied, "He knows the whole Qur'an by heart, while having a perfect command over the meaning of verses and their relation to the whole text."

"He can tell from the meaning which verse you have in mind as well as which other verses convey the same meaning.

"He can even tell you the verse's number, the page and the first verse at the top of the next page and the following other four pages. He also knows by heart the full text of several other poetry books, such as the great Iranian poets, Sa'di's Golestan, and Mohtasham Kashani's Diwan."

Age Eight Years

Giannella De Marco, on March 12, 1953, conducted the London Philharmonic Orchestra. The London concert was the 123rd of her career which began at just four years old.

World famous French composer *Olivier Messiaen* (1908-92), after teaching himself before he was eight to play the piano, then began the creation of his wonderful music.

Frederic Chopin (1810-49), who was largely a self-taught pianist, at eight years old gave his first public performance at a charity concert in Warsaw. His first extant composition was published when he was fifteen.

Age Nine Years

Daisy Ashford wrote her first and last novel, *The Young Visitors*, which sold over 200,000 copies.

Samuel Johnson (who is also mentioned above among the 3-year old prodigies), by nine years of age had read all the works of the 14th century Italian poet and scholar Petrarch. During adolescence he devoured a vast array of books, both ancient and modern, and arrived at Oxford University in 1728, when he was nineteen. He was described as "the best qualified student that had ever come there".

Conductor *Sarah Caldwell* (born 1924), American opera director and conductor. She was a child prodigy in music and mathematics, and by age nine was giving violin recitals.

Age Ten Years

Vinay Bhat (born 1965), an Indian who moved with his family to California, where he was educated. At 10 years of age he became the youngest chess master in the world.

Hikaru Nakamura (born 1988), a Japanese boy, when he was 10 became the youngest person ever to be made a chess master (he was a few months younger than Vinay Bhat).

Fats Domino (born 1923), US rhythm and blues pianist and singer, by ten years of age was already a professional performer.

The German pianist and composer *Felix Mendelssohn* (1809-47) made his first public appearance and performed his first original compositions when he was ten years old.

Age Eleven Years

The Russian composer and pianist *Dmitri Shostakovich* (1906-75) when he was eleven performed Bach's entire *Well-Tempered Clavier*.

Earl Vickers, an American, won the Grand Prize trophy in his 6th-grade science fair for a totally bogus theory of atomic structure. The next year he disproved his own theory, but only won an Honourable Mention.

When someone in 1996 asked her to "define a second", *Ruth Davies* of England at once replied – "One second equals 9,192,631,717 cycles of radiation, corresponding to the transition between the two hyperfine levels of the ground state of the caesium 133 atom." She started reading at about 6 months, word processing at two, wrote a book at four, insisted on studying algebra at nine, and began a university course on psychology at ten. By the same age she could play the trumpet and the piano, and had written a sheaf of fine poetry. (From *The Guardian.*)

French thinker, scientist and mathematician *Blaise Pascal* (1623-62), forbidden by his father to begin studying any subject until he was deemed old enough to understand it, by the age of eleven had in secret worked out for himself the first 23 propositions of *Euclid's Elements*.

Age Twelve Years

Mathematician *Carl Witte* received his Ph.D.

German philosopher and mathematician *Gottfried Wilhelm von Leibniz* (1646-1716) by the time he was twelve had taught himself Latin and Greek in order to read the books in his father's library.

Norwegian chess player *Magnus Carlsen* became the then world's youngest grand master of chess when he won the Dubai Open at the age of 13 years and 3 months.

Sergey Karjakin, on August 20, 2002, at the international tournament in Sudak, shocked the chess world by becoming the youngest grand master in chess history, at the age of 12 years and 7 months.

One story about the great 19th century Baptist preacher *CH Spurgeon* tells how as a student in early schooling, he grasped a subject so quickly his teacher simply gave him a book and told him to go outside and sit under the large tree and read!

Spurgeon was what we now call a "speed-reader" and also possessed a "photographic memory". It is said that a gentleman once brought several large books to Spurgeon and asked him to read them as a "test". After a few days, the gentleman would return and ask questions about the contents of the books. To his amazement, Spurgeon could not be "stumped" by a single question! Even years after he had read a book, he could practically quote page after page, seldom missing a word! He had the gift of "instant recall" and he was able to take a bare sketch of a sermon outline into the pulpit. (From a report on *The Spurgeon Collection*, which is housed in the library of the *William Jewell College*, in Liberty, Missouri.)

ON THE APPEARANCE OF CHRIST

The heretic Celsus, reflecting popular superstition, argued that Jesus could not have been the Son of God because he lacked the prodigious qualities an incarnate deity would have displayed (remember the stories about Caitanya, and the apocryphal stories about Jesus). By contrast, said Celsus, far from resembling a superman, Jesus had a mean appearance –

> Since a divine Spirit inhabited the body (of Jesus), it must certainly have been different from that of other beings, in respect of grandeur, or beauty, or strength, or voice, or impressiveness, or persuasiveness. For it is impossible that he, to whom was imparted some divine quality beyond other beings, should not differ from others; whereas this person did not differ in any respect from another, but was, as they report, little and ill-favoured, and ignoble.

Origen denied Celsus on both counts. Jesus was not a superman, because he had to be an ordinary man to fulfil scripture; but neither was Jesus "little" or "ignoble", although, to the spiritually blind (said Origen), he may have appeared ill-favoured ...

> (for Isaiah) prophesied regarding him that he would come and visit the multitude, not in comeliness of form, not in any surpassing beauty – "Lord, who hath believed our report, and to whom was the arm of the Lord revealed?

He made announcement before him, as a child, as a root in thirsty ground. He has no form nor glory, and we beheld him, and he had no form nor beauty; but his form was without honour, and inferior to that of the sons of men." These passages, then, Celsus listened to, because he thought they were of use to him in bringing a charge against Jesus; but he paid no attention to the words of the 45th Psalm, and why it is there said, "Gird thy sword upon thy thigh, O most mighty, with thy comeliness and beauty; and continue, and prosper, and reign."

St. Jerome, also, appealed to *Psalm 45* to prove that Christ was unusually handsome and majestic in his appearance.

JESUS OF NAZARETH

Two further affirmations need to be made about the life of Jesus.

- It was always possible for him, as it is for us, to receive direct and supernatural revelation from God by the agency of the Holy Spirit; (cp. Lu 9:47; Jn 1:47-49; 4:16-19.
- It must be allowed that "normal" attainment for Jesus, whose faculties were unclouded by sin, must have been much higher than what is normal for us (especially in spiritual matters), upon whose faculties sin has had a devastating effect.

Hence the story in *Luke 2:46-47* probably does not have any supernatural content; it simply reflects the clear perceptions of an intelligent boy who was free of sin, and who had an unsullied love for God (cp. the examples given above of child prodigies). The fact that Jesus, at 12 years of age, was becoming aware of his true identity and mission does not require either a miracle, some improbable innate self-awareness, nor even remarkable precocity. Rather, it may be attributed to what he had heard about the circumstances of his birth, and to his deepening understanding of scripture. Through prayer and the guidance of the Holy Spirit it seems that the realisation was growing in him that he was the one of whom the prophets had spoken. It is unlikely that he had a full grasp of his true identity until several years later, and perhaps not until the day of his baptism (Mt 3:16-17).

ISIS AND OSIRIS

You may find this piece of Egyptian mythology interesting.

According to the ancient Egyptians, Osiris was a long-ago king who was married to his sister Isis. When he first arrived in Egypt, Osiris found the land in a state of chaotic barbarity. He imposed upon the people a body of just laws, and established among them commerce, industry, religion, and other elements of a civilised society. He had a brother Seth who greatly envied the growing power and prosperity of Osiris, and determined to seize the throne for himself. He murdered Osiris by persuading him to step into a golden coffin, whereupon the lid was slammed shut, fastened, and the coffin thrown into the Nile.

Isis rescued the body of her husband, but Seth forcibly took it from her, tore it into 14 pieces, and scattered them far and wide across the land of Egypt.

The grieving Isis bound herself by a sworn oath to find all the pieces and to bring them together for burial in one hallowed place. She searched patiently, refusing to be daunted, overcame all obstacles, and eventually succeeded. She placed the pieces together, turned herself into a kite, and furiously beating her wings above the remains, breathed life back into the broken flesh. Many Egyptian pictures show a coffin or burial place embraced by the wings of Isis, expressing the mourners' confidence that those enfolding wings will convey eternal life to the one buried there.

As the wings of Isis were stirring the air, the soul of Osiris emerged from the gathered pieces, and reunited with his wife. She conceived and later bore a son, Horus. In the meantime Osiris was compelled to resume his journey to the underworld, where he was destined to become the god of all the dead.

Seth remained upon the throne until Horus grew up and vowed that he would avenge his father. After years of bitter warfare the young man triumphed, put his uncle to death, and regained the throne, until he was called to fulfil his own destiny by becoming the god of the daytime and of light and goodness. His successors on Egypt's throne, until the end of the monarchy in Roman times, 2,000 years later, were worshipped as embodiments of Horus seated upon the Horus Throne.

After she died, Isis was proclaimed goddess of the night, the great "Mother Goddess", and was reckoned to be powerful in magic. Her cult was immensely popular, soon spreading far beyond Egypt, so that she was still being worshipped as late as 500 years after the resurrection of Christ.

The myth of the life, death, and renewed life of Osiris was profoundly believed. Well into the Christian era, it remained the primary source of the ancient Egyptian assurance (which was shared by everyone in the land, from high-born to low) of eternal life. But its mythical and bizarre elements separate it altogether from the sober eyewitness accounts given in the gospels of the birth, life, death, and resurrection of Christ.

Yet the Egyptian myths do expose the universal human hunger for the very things promised in the gospel, which has truly abolished death and brought life, light, and immortality to all who believe in Christ (2 Ti 1:10).

THE EMPEROR AS "SAVIOUR"

In his book *The Romans and their Gods in the Age of Augustus*, R. M. Ogilvie writes –

> Above all, a god is a saviour. Yet there were many men who could legitimately claim to have saved more of their fellow-men than any god. The successors of Alexander the Great were regularly hailed as Saviours (σωτηρες), and the idea was by no means foreign to Republican Rome. Marius Gratidianus, praetor in 86 B.C., who carried out some popular currency reforms, was greeted with a spontaneous demonstration in which statues of him were set up throughout the city and honoured with incense and wine as a Saviour god. What was tolerated for an ephemeral benefactor like Gratidianus was a thousand times more justifiable in the case of a ruler like Augustus. Velleius Paterculus, an officer under Tiberius who turned to history in his retirement, eloquently captured the spirit of men's emotions at that time (II.89) – "There was nothing that men could ask of gods, nothing that gods could offer to men, nothing that prayer could conceive of, nothing that ultimate bliss could achieve, which was not vouchsafed to the state, to the people, to the world by Augustus after his return to Rome." There indeed was a man who gave gifts worthy of a

god, as Propertius summed it up (IV, 6, 36) – *mundi servitor*, Saviour of the World. [126]

VERONICA'S STATUE OF CHRIST

In Christian legend, the name of the woman whom Jesus cured of a perpetual haemorrhage was Veronica (Mt 9:20-22; Mk 5:25; Lu 8:43) –

> The story is told ... how Jesus stumbled under the weight of his cross on the way to his crucifixion, and a woman stepped out of the crowd and wiped the sweat from his face. After he had moved on, she found that his features were imprinted on the ... cloth ... which she had used. This relic ... has been in Rome since the 8th century. It is now in a chapel in the crypt of St Peter's and is one of the three sacred relics (the others being St Longinus' spear and a piece of the True Cross) which are exhibited on great festivals. ...
>
> In the *Golden Legend* there is another version of the story ... (The) emperor Tiberius, who suffered from a distressing malady, had heard of Jesus and learned that he cured all ills. He sent an officer named Volusianus to Pilate to ask for Jesus to be transported to Rome. Pilate, terrified because he had crucified the miracle-worker, begged for a short delay. In the meantime Volusianus had discovered an old woman named Veronica who told him how the face of Jesus had been imprinted on her linen kerchief. She refused to sell the relic, but

---

[126] WW Norton & Co. Inc., New York, 1969; pg. 120.

accompanied Volusianus to Rome. When Tiberius looked on the Holy Face, he was cured. [127]

She remained (according to the legend) in Rome, and upon her death she bequeathed the cloth to Pope St Clement and his successors, and this is presumed by many to be the relic that now resides in St Peter's.

Long before this, after she had been cured of her flux, Veronica, so we are told, returned home, recouped her spent fortune, and in gratitude for what the Lord had done, erected a statue in honour of Christ. The 4th century historian Eusebius claims to have seen the statue. But not long after, when Julian came to the throne, it was pulled down. Sozoment describes it thus –

> Among so many remarkable events which occurred during the reign of Julian, I must not omit to mention one which affords a sign of the power of Christ, and proof of the Divine wrath against the emperor.
>
> Having heard that at Caesarea Philippi, otherwise called Paneas, a city of Phoenicia, there was a celebrated statue of Christ which had been erected by a woman whom the Lord had cured of a flow of blood, Julian

---

[127] Dictionary of Christian Law and Legend, compiled by JCJ Metford, Thames and Hudson, London, 1983; article Veronica, St. The primary origin of the story is an apocryphal work, The Gospel of Nicodemus – "And a certain woman Veronica crying out from afar off said – '[I had an issue of blood and touched the hem of his garment, and the flowing of my blood was stayed which I had twelve years.' The Jews say – 'We have a law that a woman shall not come to give testimony.' (Part One, VII)

commanded it to be taken down and a statue of himself erected in its place; but a violent fire from heaven fell upon (the emperor's statue) and broke off the parts contiguous to the breast; the head and neck were thrown prostrate, and it was transfixed to the ground with the face downwards at the point where the fracture of the bust was; and it has stood in that fashion from that day until now, full of the rust of the lightning. The statue of Christ was dragged around the city and mutilated by the pagans; but the Christians recovered the fragments, and deposited the statue in the church in which it is still preserved. Eusebius relates, that at the base of this statue grew an herb which was unknown to the physicians and empirics, but was efficacious in the cure of all disorders. It does not appear a matter of astonishment to me, that, after God had vouchsafed to dwell with men, he should condescend to bestow benefits upon them. [128]

This is the passage from *Eusebius* mentioned by Sozomen just above –

Since I have mentioned this city (Paneas) I do not think it proper to omit an account which is worthy of record for posterity. For they say that the woman with an issue of blood, who, as we learn from the sacred Gospel, received from our Saviour deliverance from her affliction, came from this place, and that her house is shown in the city, and that remarkable

---

[128] Ecclesiastical History, V, 21

memorials of the kindness of the Saviour to her remain there. For there stands upon an elevated pedestal, by the gates of her house, a brazen image of a woman kneeling, with her hands stretched out, as if she were praying. Opposite this is another upright image of a man, made of the same material, clothed decently in a double cloak, and extending his hand toward the woman. At his feet, beside the statue itself, is a certain strange plant, which climbs up to the hem of the brazen cloak, and is a remedy for all kinds of diseases. They say that this statue is an image of Jesus. It has remained to our day, so that we ourselves also saw it when we were staying in the city. Nor is it strange that those of the Gentiles who, of old, were benefited by our Saviour, should have done such things, since we have learned also that the likenesses of his apostles Paul and Peter, and of Christ himself, are preserved in paintings, the ancients being accustomed, as it is likely, according to a habit of the Gentiles, to pay this kind of honour indiscriminately to those regarded by them as deliverers. [129]

THE QUR'AN (KORAN)

The Qur'an disdains the need of miracles to establish the existence of God and of his benign providence. The Bible, too, echoes such ideas (Ps 19:1-4; Ro 1:19-21; etc), but then, in gracious condescension to our need, not only contains a record of many stunning miracles, but promises that they will be an ongoing part of walking with God. In this way, the

---

[129] Church History, Bk. 7, Ch. 18.

Bible risks all, for if the record and the promise should fail, then its other claims must also be falsified. But on the contrary, the experience of the people of God has verified every biblical claim.

Here are some relevant Suras from the Qur'an –

JONAH [10:20]   People say to the Prophet, "How is it that no miracle has come down to you from your Lord?" But the Prophet says, "The future belongs to GOD; so wait, and I too will wait along with you."

LIVESTOCK [6:157-158]   People say, "If only a scripture could come down to us, we would be better guided than our forefathers." But a proven scripture has come down to you from your Lord, and a beacon, and a mercy. Now, who is more evil than one who rejects these proofs from God, and disregards them? ... Are they waiting for the angels to come to them, or the Lord himself, or some physical manifestation of the Lord? The day that happens no soul will benefit from it if that soul did not believe before that day!

KNEELING [45:2-5]   The heavens and the earth are full of proofs for those who are ready to believe. Indeed, your very creation, and the creation of all the animals, provide sufficient proofs for people who open their eyes. Also, the alternating nights and days, and the provisions that GOD sends down from the sky to revive the dead land, and the ever-shifting winds -- all these are proofs for those who are willing to understand.

THE ROMANS [30:20-25]   Among His proofs is that He created you from dust, then you became reproducing humans. Among His proofs is that He created for you spouses from among yourselves, in order to have tranquility and contentment with each other, and He placed in your hearts love and care towards your spouses. In this, there are sufficient proofs for people who think. Among His proofs are the creation of the heavens and the earth, and the variations in your languages and your colors. In these, there are signs for the knowledgeable. Among His proofs is your sleeping during the night or the day, and your working in pursuit of His provisions. In this, there are sufficient proofs for people who can hear. Among His proofs is that He shows you the lightning as a source of fear, as well as hope, then He sends down from the sky water to revive a land that has been dead. In these, there are sufficient proofs for people who understand. Among His proofs is that the heaven and the earth are standing at His disposal. Finally, when He calls you out of the earth, one call, you will surely at once come out from your grave.

THE "SEVENTY WEEKS"

Consider the astonishing miracle of the prophecy found in *Daniel* (9:24-27).

The prophecy deals with *"70 weeks"*, which are usually taken to represent 490 years (70x7), divided into three groups, thus –

- 7 weeks = 49 years
- 62 weeks = 434 years
- 1 week = 7 years

The main ideas are –

<u>The Jewish captivity in Babylon was to end</u> (vs. 1-23), and a command given for the people to return to Palestine, and to rebuild Jerusalem and the Temple (vs. 25). This restoration of Israel was to take place during a period of "70 sevens" (= 490 years), which would begin with the issuing of a "decree" (vs.25) –

- Many dates for that decree have been suggested, but the most common are linked with two announcements concerning the Jews that were made by <u>Artaxerxes</u> in the 7th and 20th years of his reign, namely, 457 BC (Ezr 7:7 ff), and 445 BC (Ne 2:1-8).

- From the date of the decree to rebuild Jerusalem, 490 years would elapse until the time when the messiah would come and be *"cut off"*.
- During the first 49 years, the streets and walls of the city would be rebuilt, though the times would be *"troubled"* (see *Ezra* and *Nehemiah*).
- Following this, another 62 weeks (= 434 years) would elapse before the appearance of the Messiah; which leads to the following calculations (among other possible variations) –

    457 BC + 483 solar years = 27 AD
    445 BC + 483 lunar years = 32 AD

- Given the fact that authorities differ by as much as 10 years in the date when they reckon Christ began his public ministry, the above dates represent a miracle of accurate prophecy.

"*After*" the *"69th week"* (that is, after 481 years) the Messiah would be *"cut off, but not for himself"* – a vision of the cross, which again was wonderfully fulfilled.

A great war would begin (vs. 26,27b) –

- *"the prince"* was Titus, and the prophecy was basically fulfilled in 70 AD, except that *"war"* and *"desolation"* are to continue until *"the end"* (of the age) (cp Mt 24:15-16; Lu 21:20-24).

There are other ways of understanding the oracle, but the outline above seems to me to be the best way of looking at it, and also the one that is most consistent with other scriptures.

CHRIST THE LORD

Dr Barry Chant created the following list of interchanges between "Lord", "Christ", and "God" –

Philippians 2:11. Jesus Christ is called Lord, and this is to the glory of God; that is, to identify Jesus as Yahweh is not blasphemy, but actually honouring to God.

1 Corinthians 2:8. The "Lord of Glory" was crucified. If that title is taken in isolation, it would appear to refer to God (cp. Ex 24:16). But this "Lord of Glory" is crucified, so he must be Christ.

2 Timothy 4:8. The term *"the Lord, the righteous Judge,"* appears to refer to God; but the remainder of the verse refers to *"his appearing"* – that is to the second advent; thus it actually means Christ. (See also vs. 17,18,22.)

2 Peter 3:8-10. Those verses are usually taken to refer to God. But look at 1:11; 2:20; 3:18; etc. There *Christ* is called the *Lord*. Either Peter is being very careless, or he sees God and Christ as one.

Philippians 3:8. (plus 1 Th 4:15-18; 2 Th 3:5; 1 Co 3:20; 7:22; 2 Co 5:11). In those references *Lord* is used interchangeably of Christ and God, thus showing their mutual identity. In the same way, just as *Lord* is freely applied to both the Father and the Son, so also in the NT the terms *God* and *Christ* are often used interchangeably. Thus – forgiveness is from God (Cl 2:13) or from Christ (3:13); revelation is from God (Ga 1:16) or from Christ (1:12); churches are of God or of Christ (Ro 16:16; 1 Th 2:14); the judgment seat is of God or of Christ (Ro 14:10-12; 2 Co 5:10). See also Ja 1:1; Ro 1:1; Re 22:3; etc. It is clear that to the NT writers there was no essential difference between saying that a gift came from God or from Christ. To them, *Jesus was God*.

THE SAINTS OF OLD

There are numerous accounts of the ferocious privations that various hermits, monks, and others, both men and women, inflicted upon themselves in an effort to achieve a higher level of merit with God, or perhaps even just to be sure of their salvation.

They all demonstrate the futility of any attempt to build some righteousness of our own; they show the folly of refusing (like the ancient Jews) to submit to the righteousness of God (Ro 10:3). The fact is unassailable – we must be content to rest solely and entirely upon the grace of God, resisting all attempts to add something to the completed work of Christ.

Because the tragic people in the stories below failed to grasp the true meaning of the gospel, because they never truly understood the grace of God, they were driven to buy some credit in heaven by their good works and sacrifices. They failed dismally. We must be saved by grace alone, apart from any work of ours, or we will never be saved at all.

ACEPSEMUS (5TH CENTURY)

> Immuring himself in a cell, he persevered for 60 years, neither being seen nor speaking . . . He received the food that was brought to him by stretching his hand through a small hole. To prevent his being exposed to those who wished to see him, the hole was not dug straight

through the thickness of the wall, but obliquely, being made in the shape of a curve. (130)

- the food brought to him was mainly lentils soaked in water
- at the end of 60 years he emerged, bent double under a weight of iron (which he had apparently borne throughout the entire period)
- he looked so wild and shaggy, that he was once actually taken for a wolf by a shepherd, who assailed him with stones, till he discovered his error, and then worshipped the hermit as a saint
- he declared that God had shown him that he would die within a few weeks (which happened).
- but just before then "he was allowed to study for the priesthood, underwent training, and was ordained, dying in a state of happiness just shortly after entering the priesthood." (131)

BARADATUS (5TH CENT.)

I wish to record the life of the wonderful Baradatus, for he too devised new tests of endurance. First, immuring himself for a long time in a cell, he enjoyed divine consolation alone. From there, aspiring to the ridge situated above, and constructing out of wood a small chest that did not even match his body, in

---

(130) Theodoret, Religious History #15; tr. by R. M. Price, A History of the Monks of Syria, Cistercian Publications, Kalamazoo, Michigan, 1985; pg. 114-116.

(131) See St Acepsimas, under the list of saints at www.catholic.org, where it is spelled "Acepsimus".

this he dwelt, obliged to stoop the whole time – for its length was not equal in size to the height of his body. It was not even fitted together with planks, but had openings like a lattice . . . (so that) he was neither safe from the assault of the rains nor free from the flames of the sun, but endured both of them like the other open-air ascetics, whom he surpassed only in the labour of reclusion.

Having spent a long time in this way he later came out . . . (but now) he stands all the time, stretching out his hands and hymning the God of the universe, and covering his entire body with a tunic of skins – only round the nose and mouth has he left a small opening for breath, in order to receive and inhale the common air, since otherwise human nature cannot live. He endures all this labour, even though with a body not robust but much afflicted by numerous ailments; but his bubbling zeal, inflamed by divine love, compels to labour one who cannot labour." [132]

THALELAEUS

- he made a kind of cylinder out of two cart wheels joined by planks and suspended in the air on chains
- after he had been squatting in his "bucket" for ten years he was visited by Theodoret, who says that he was unable to straighten himself and "always sits bent

---

[132] Ibid. #27.

double, with his forehead pressed against his knee" (133)

- it is not known how much longer he remained there.

OTHERS

Theodoret describes other monks who lived in tiny huts or cells in which they could neither stand nor lie down full length, while others lived in disused cisterns, or dug deep holes in which they immured themselves –

- One hermit lived alone in a cave on the top of a mountain, and never once turned his face toward the west.
- Such men became a pattern for many others who locked themselves alone in caves for life, slept on beds of thorns, laced their food with bitter herbs, twisted thorns and thistles into their garments, burdened themselves with massive loads of iron, etc.

Then there were ***James*** and ***Alexander*** of Cyr, who (like Baradatus) imposed upon themselves the sentence of standing in the open for the rest of their lives. [134]

They too were copied by others, who stood in the open, sometimes for many years, using various tethers or props to hold themselves upright.

Sulpitius Severus tells of a hermit who for fifty years lived secluded from all human society, in the clefts of Mount Sinai, entirely destitute of clothing, and all overgrown with thick hair, avoiding every visitor, because, as he said, intercourse with men interrupted the visits of the angels.

---

[133] Ibid. #28.
[134] Theodoret, Ecclesiastical History, 17-21.

One of the most renowned hermits was **_St Simeon Stylites_** (390-459) who sat on a 60-foot pillar for 36 years. I will return to him; but in the meantime note that he was outdone by **_St Simeon the Younger_** –

- the early historian **_Evagrius_** ("Ecclesiastical History") says that while Simeon was still a child he befriended and tamed a young panther, which he led to a nearby monastery – the preceptor, who was ensconced on a column saw in this a sign of special sanctity and invited the boy to join him on his column

- this Simeon agreed to do, and then spent the next 68 years on pillars of ever-increasing height, including 45 years on his last, during which many miracles of healing, exorcisms, fulfilled prophecies, and the like, were attributed to him

- but both Simeons (the elder and younger) were exceeded by **_St Alipius_**, who combined the idea of standing with that of a pillar, and so stood on his pillar for 53 years, until he lost the use of both his feet, upon which he spent his last 14 years lying only on one side of his body. He is revered as the patron of infertile women and is usually portrayed as an old man on a pillar, holding a baby.

Evagrius writes further – [135]

> (There are some) who individually seclude themselves in chambers of so limited a height and width that they can neither stand upright nor lie down at ease, confining their existence to "dens and caves of the earth", as says the

---

[135] Ecclesiastical History; Bohn's Ecclesiastical Library; London, 1854; pg 285, 286.

apostle. Some too take up their dwelling with the wild beasts . . . Another mode has also been devised, one which reaches to the utmost extent of resolution and endurance; for transporting themselves to a scorched wilderness, and covering only those parts which nature requires to be concealed, both men and women leave the rest of their persons exposed both to excessive frosts and scorching blasts, regardless alike of heat and cold. They, moreover, cast off the ordinary food of mankind, and feed upon the produce of the ground, whence they are termed Grazers, allowing themselves no more than is barely sufficient to sustain life. . . . I will mention still another class . . . persons who, when by virtue they have attained to a condition exempt from passion, return to the world. . . . They (then) frequent the public baths, mostly mingling and bathing with women, since they have attained to such an ascendancy over their passions as to possess dominion over nature, and neither by sight, touch, or even embracing of the female, to relapse into their natural condition. It (is) their desire to be men and among men and women among women, and to participate in both sexes. In short, by a life thus all excellent and divine, virtue exercises a sovereignty in opposition to nature . . .

Consider also **_Cyprian_** –

Cyprian de Mulverton, fifth prior of the monastery of Saint Francis, a prelate of singular sanctity . . . vowed never again to behold with earthly eyes the blessed light of heaven, nor to dwell longer with his fellow men.... He kept his vow. Out of the living rock that sustained the saintly structure, beneath the chapel of the monastery, was another chapel wrought, and thither, after bidding an eternal farewell to the world ... the holy man retired.

... Ascetic to the severest point to which nature's endurance could be stretched, Cyprian even denied himself repose. He sought not sleep, and knew it only when it stole on him unawares. His couch was the flinty rock; and long afterwards, when the zealous resorted to the sainted prior's cell, and were shown those sharp and jagged stones, they marvelled how one like unto themselves could rest, or even recline upon their points without anguish.... His limbs were clothed in a garb of horsehair of the coarsest fabric; his drink was the dank drops that oozed out of the porous walls of his cell; and his sustenance, such morsels as were bestowed upon him by the poor.... No fire was suffered, where perpetual winter reigned. None were admitted to his nightly vigils; none witnessed any act of penance; nor were any groans heard to issue from that dreary cave; but the knotted blood-stained thong, discovered near his couch, too plainly betrayed in what manner those long nights were spent. [136]

---

[136] The above quote comes from W. H. Ainsworth's novel <u>Rookwood</u>, Book III, Ch. 10 (1834), which also contains a vivid description of the famous ride from London to York by the highwayman Dick Turpin on his mare Black Bess (although it seems that the rider was actually another highwayman who lived a century earlier).

Likewise, in the 6th century, in convents, it was not uncommon for a **_nun_** to have herself bricked into a small space, leaving only a tiny slit through which food was passed, and there remain until death. Possession of such a "living relic" brought enormous prestige to a convent, and large numbers of pilgrims.

Consider also the female saints of the Middle Ages, who walked on glass, stood naked outdoors on ice, ate only embittered food, flogged and lashed themselves mercilessly, drank pus, adopted a crucifix position and remained there unmoving for hours until their bodies over-rode their wills and they collapsed, and to those pains were added numerous other agonising and sometimes absurd self-imposed sufferings. [137]

But let me sum it all up by returning to the best known of the hermits –

ST SIMEON STYLITES (THE ELDER) –

The son of a shepherd, when a boy of thirteen years, he was powerfully affected by the beatitudes, which he heard read in the church, and betook himself to a cloister. He lay several days, without eating or drinking, before the threshold, and begged to be admitted as the meanest servant of the house. He accustomed himself to eat only once a week, on Sunday. During Lent he even went through the whole forty days without any food; a fact almost incredible even for a tropical climate. The first attempt of this kind brought him to the verge of death; but his constitution conformed itself, and when Theodoret visited him, he had solemnized six and

---

[137] They are graphically described in the book <u>Holy Feast and Holy Fast</u>, by Caroline Bynum; University of California Press, Berkeley, 1987.

twenty Lent seasons by total abstinence, and thus surpassed Moses, Elias, and even Christ, who never fasted so but once.

He remained in that monastery as a servant for two years, after which, dissatisfied with its comparative laxity he moved to a more austere monastery, where he practised harsher mortifications than any of the other inmates, until he nearly died after twisting a rope of palm leaves so tightly around his waist that it sank beneath his flesh. It took the monks three days to remove the rope by incisions after softening his skin with liquids, after which the abbot expelled him. He then spent three years chained to a rock on top of a mountain, but so many pilgrims began to climb to his retreat that, to escape them, he climbed onto the top of a stone pillar about 3 metres high. There he remained for 4 years, dependent entirely upon disciples for the meagre sustenance that was conveyed to him by a ladder.

But he found himself still too much interrupted by pilgrims, so he built a second pillar, 6 metres high, where he spent 3 years; then another, 10 metres high (10 years); and then a fourth, 18 metres high, his last, where he spent the next 20 years.

During lent he fasted absolutely, spending the first two weeks standing upright praising God; the next two sitting; and the last two (owing to growing weakness from the fast) lying horizontal. Every day he repeatedly bowed his body in prayer, prostrating himself more than 1000 times in succession, while wearing a heavy iron collar.

For a long time he suffered himself to be tormented by twenty enormous bugs, and concealed an abscess full of worms, to train himself in patience and meekness. Twice each day he preached to the multitudes who thronged at the foot of his pillar, including emperors and princes. By his prayers, so it is said, he healed the sick; and in response to his preaching thousands were converted to Christ. He wrote many influential letters and interspersed his teaching and writing with excellent theology.

His preaching is said to have been practical and compassionate and his doctrine orthodox. He died while bowing before God on his pillar –

> From his original pulpit, as a mediator between heaven and earth, he preached repentance twice a day to the astonished spectators, settled controversies, vindicated the orthodox faith, extorted laws even from an emperor, healed the sick, wrought miracles, and converted thousands of heathen, Ishmaelites, Iberians, Armenians, and Persians to Christianity, or at least to the Christian name. All this the celebrated Theodoret relates as an eyewitness during the lifetime of the saint. He terms him the great wonder of the world, and compares him to a candle on a candlestick, and to the sun itself, which sheds its rays on every side. He asks the objector to this mode of life to consider that God often uses very striking means to arouse the negligent, as the history of the prophets shows; and concludes his narrative with the remark: "Should the saint live longer, he may do yet greater wonders, for he is a universal ornament and honor of religion." He died in 459, in the sixty-ninth year of his age, of a long-concealed and loathsome ulcer on his leg; and his body was

brought in solemn procession to the metropolitan church of Antioch." [138]

Perhaps the best portrayal of the inner feelings and motives of the hermits can be found in Lord Tennyson's deeply moving and sensitive poem, *St Simeon Stylites*. Many critics think the poem is overdone, but in my opinion they are writing from a secular stand, without any sensitivity to the inner compulsions of a man driven to attain holiness by any means that he can grasp. Tennyson, it seems to me, enters fully into the heart and mind of such a person, and portrays the inner anxiety, even the agony, that must torment anyone who fails to seize the righteousness, the holiness, that is already wonderfully ours simply through faith in the completed work of Christ. Read the poem and make your own judgment –

> Altho' I be the basest of mankind,
> From scalp to sole one slough and crust of sin,
> Unfit for earth, unfit for heaven, scarce meet
> For troops of devils, mad with blasphemy,
> I will not cease to grasp the hope I hold
> Of saintdom, and to clamour, mourn and sob,
> Battering the gates of heaven with storms of prayer,
> Have mercy, Lord, and take away my sin.
>
> Let this avail, just, dreadful, mighty God,
> This not be all in vain that thrice ten years,
> Thrice multiplied by superhuman pangs,
> In hungers and in thirsts, fevers and cold,
> In coughs, aches, stitches, ulcerous throes and cramps,
> A sign betwixt the meadow and the cloud,

---

[138] From Philip Schaff – <u>History of the Church</u>. I gathered the other details of the life of Simeon from various sources.

      Patient on this tall pillar I have borne
Rain, wind, frost, heat, hail, damp, and sleet, and snow;
      And I had hoped that ere this period closed
      Thou wouldst have caught me up into Thy rest,
      Denying not these weather-beaten limbs
      The meed of saints, the white robe and the palm.
      O take the meaning, Lord: I do not breathe,
      Not whisper, any murmur of complaint.
      Pain heap'd ten-hundred-fold to this, were still
      Less burthen, by ten-hundred-fold, to bear,
Than were those lead-like tons of sin, that crush'd
      My spirit flat before thee.

      O Lord, Lord,
Thou knowest I bore this better at the first,
      For I was strong and hale of body then;
      And tho' my teeth, which now are dropt away,
      Would chatter with the cold, and all my beard
      Was tagg'd with icy fringes in the moon,
I drown'd the whoopings of the owl with sound
      Of pious hymns and psalms, and sometimes saw
      An angel stand and watch me, as I sang.
Now am I feeble grown; my end draws nigh;
      I hope my end draws nigh: half deaf I am,
      So that I scarce can hear the people hum
About the column's base, and almost blind,
And scarce can recognise the fields I know;
      And both my thighs are rotted with the dew;
      Yet cease I not to clamour and to cry,
While my stiff spine can hold my weary head,
Till all my limbs drop piecemeal from the stone,
      Have mercy, mercy: take away my sin.

      O Jesus, if thou wilt not save my soul,
Who may be saved? who is it may be saved?
Who may be made a saint, if I fail here?

Show me the man hath suffered more than I.
For did not all thy martyrs die one death?
For either they were stoned, or crucified,
Or burn'd in fire, or boil'd in oil, or sawn
In twain beneath the ribs; but I die here
To-day, and whole years long, a life of death.
Bear witness, if I could have found a way
(And heedfully I sifted all my thought)
More slowly-painful to subdue this home
Of sin, my flesh, which I despise and hate,
I had not stinted practice, O my God.

For not alone this pillar-punishment,
Not this alone I bore: but while I lived
In the white convent down the valley there,
For many weeks about my loins I wore
The rope that haled the buckets from the well,
Twisted as tight as I could knot the noose;
And spake not of it to a single soul,
Until the ulcer, eating thro' my skin,
Betray'd my secret penance, so that all
My brethren marvell'd greatly. More than this
I bore, whereof, O God, thou knowest all.

Three winters, that my soul might grow to thee,
I lived up there on yonder mountain side.
My right leg chain'd into the crag, I lay
Pent in a roofless close of ragged stones;
Inswathed sometimes in wandering mist, and twice
Black'd with thy branding thunder, and sometimes
Sucking the damps for drink, and eating not,
Except the spare chance-gift of those that came
To touch my body and be heal'd, and live:
And they say then that I work'd miracles,
Whereof my fame is loud amongst mankind,
Cured lameness, palsies, cancers. Thou, O God,

Knowest alone whether this was or no.
Have mercy, mercy; cover all my sin.

Then, that I might be more alone with thee,
Three years I lived upon a pillar, high
Six cubits, and three years on one of twelve;
And twice three years I crouch'd on one that rose
Twenty by measure; last of all, I grew
Twice ten long weary weary years to this,
That numbers forty cubits from the soil.
I think that I have borne as much as this--
Or else I dream--and for so long a time,
If I may measure time by yon slow light,
And this high dial, which my sorrow crowns--
So much--even so.

And yet I know not well,
For that the evil ones come here, and say,
"Fall down, O Simeon: thou hast suffer'd long
For ages and for ages!" then they prate
Of penances I cannot have gone thro',
Perplexing me with lies; and oft I fall,
Maybe for months, in such blind lethargies,
That Heaven, and Earth, and Time are choked. But yet

Bethink thee, Lord, while thou and all the saints
Enjoy themselves in Heaven, and men on earth
House in the shade of comfortable roofs,
Sit with their wives by fires, eat wholesome food,
And wear warm clothes, and even beasts have stalls,
I, 'tween the spring and downfall of the light,
Bow down one thousand and two hundred times,
To Christ, the Virgin Mother, and the Saints;
Or in the night, after a little sleep,
I wake: the chill stars sparkle; I am wet
With drenching dews, or stiff with crackling frost.

I wear an undress'd goatskin on my back;
A grazing iron collar grinds my neck;
And in my weak, lean arms I lift the cross,
And strive and wrestle with thee till I die:
O mercy, mercy! wash away my sin.

O Lord, thou knowest what a man I am;
A sinful man, conceived and born in sin.
'Tis their own doing; this is none of mine;
Lay it not to me. Am I to blame for this,
That here come those that worship me? Ha! ha!
They think that I am somewhat. What am I?
The silly people take me for a saint,
And bring me offerings of fruit and flowers:
And I, in truth (thou wilt bear witness here)
Have all in all endured as much, and more
Than many just and holy men, whose names
Are register'd and calendar'd for saints.

Good people, you do ill to kneel to me.
What is it I can have done to merit this?
I am a sinner viler than you all.
It may be I have wrought some miracles,
And cured some halt and maim'd; but what of that?
It may be, no one, even among the saints,
May match his pains with mine; but what of that?
Yet do not rise: for you may look on me,
And in your looking you may kneel to God.
Speak! is there any of you halt or maim'd?
I think you know I have some power with Heaven
From my long penance: let him speak his wish.

Yes, I can heal him. Power goes forth from me.
They say that they are heal'd. Ah, hark! they shout
"St. Simeon Stylites". Why, if so,
God reaps a harvest in me. O my soul,

God reaps a harvest in thee. If this be,
Can I work miracles and not be saved?
This is not told of any. They were saints.
It cannot be but that I shall be saved;
Yea, crown'd a saint. They shout, "Behold a saint!"
And lower voices saint me from above.
Courage, St. Simeon! This dull chrysalis
Cracks into shining wings, and hope ere death
Spreads more and more and more, that God hath now
Sponged and made blank of crimeful record all
My mortal archives.

O my sons, my sons,
I, Simeon of the pillar, by surname
Stylites, among men; I, Simeon,
The watcher on the column till the end;
I, Simeon, whose brain the sunshine bakes;
I, whose bald brows in silent hours become
Unnaturally hoar with rime, do now
From my high nest of penance here proclaim
That Pontius and Iscariot by my side
Show'd like fair seraphs. On the coals I lay,
A vessel full of sin: all hell beneath
Made me boil over. Devils pluck'd my sleeve;
Abaddon and Asmodeus caught at me.
I smote them with the cross; they swarm'd again.
In bed like monstrous apes they crush'd my chest:
They flapp'd my light out as I read: I saw
Their faces grow between me and my book:
With colt-like whinny and with hoggish whine
They burst my prayer. Yet this way was left,
And by this way I'scaped them. Mortify
Your flesh, like me, with scourges and with thorns;
Smite, shrink not, spare not. If it may be, fast
Whole Lents, and pray. I hardly, with slow steps,
With slow, faint steps, and much exceeding pain,

Have scrambled past those pits of fire, that still
Sing in mine ears. But yield not me the praise:
God only thro' his bounty hath thought fit,
Among the powers and princes of this world,
To make me an example to mankind,
Which few can reach to. Yet I do not say
But that a time may come--yea, even now,
Now, now, his footsteps smite the threshold stairs
Of life--I say, that time is at the doors
When you may worship me without reproach;
For I will leave my relics in your land,
And you may carve a shrine about my dust,
And burn a fragrant lamp before my bones,
When I am gather'd to the glorious saints.

While I spake then, a sting of shrewdest pain
Ran shrivelling thro' me, and a cloudlike change,
In passing, with a grosser film made thick
These heavy, horny eyes. The end! the end!
Surely the end! What's here? a shape, a shade,
A flash of light. Is that the angel there
That holds a crown? Come, blessed brother, come,
I know thy glittering face. I waited long;
My brows are ready. What! deny it now?
Nay, draw, draw, draw nigh. So I clutch it. Christ!
'Tis gone: 'tis here again; the crown! the crown!
So now 'tis fitted on and grows to me,
And from it melt the dews of Paradise,
Sweet! sweet! spikenard, and balm, and frankincense.
Ah! let me not be fool'd, sweet saints: I trust
That I am whole, and clean, and meet for Heaven.

Speak, if there be a priest, a man of God,
Among you there, and let him presently
Approach, and lean a ladder on the shaft,
And climbing up into my airy home,

Deliver me the blessed sacrament;
For by the warning of the Holy Ghost,
I prophesy that I shall die to-night,
A quarter before twelve.

But thou, O Lord,
Aid all this foolish people; let them take
Example, pattern: lead them to thy light.

BIBLIOGRAPHY

BOOKS

Ainsworth, W. H. *Rookwood*. (1834).

Aubrey, John. Richard Barber, editor. *Brief Lives*. London Folio Society: 1975.

Barnes, Albert. *Notes on the Psalms*. Gall and Inglis: London.

Bhaktivedanta, A. C., Swami Prabhupada. *Srimad Bhagavatam*. Translation and commentary published 1970 by the International Society for Krishna Consciousness, New York.

Blake, William. *The Everlasting Gospel* (c. 1810).

Bohn. *Ecclesiastical History*. Bohn's Ecclesiastical Library: 1977 edition.

Boswell, J. *Life of Johnson*. (1747).

Bryson, Bill. *A Short History of Nearly Everything*. Pub. Black Swan: 2003.

Bunyan, John. *Pilgrim's Progress*. (1678).

Bynum, Caroline. *Holy Feast and Holy Fast*. University of California Press: Berkeley, 1987.

Chant, Ken. *Strong Reasons*. Vision Publishing, Ramona CA.

Clough, A. H. Tr. *Lives of the Noble Grecians and Romans*. (Plutarch. c. 46-120)

Dawood, N. J. Tr. *The Koran*. Penguin Classics: 1980.

Douglas, J. D. Editor. *The New International Dictionary of the Christian Church*. Zondervan Corporation: Grand Rapids, 1978.

Fox, Robin Lane. *Alexander the Great*. Folio Society: London, 1997.

Hastings, James. Editor. *Dictionary of the New Testament*. Reprint by Baker Book House: Grand Rapids, Michigan, 1973.

Herman, Nicholas. Donald Attwater, tr. *The Practice of the Presence of God*. Burns and Oates: London, 1977.

Macaulay, G. C., tr. (c. 1900) *The History*. (Herodotus, c. BC 480-420).

Hill, Robert W. Jnr, editor. *Tennyson's Poetry*. W.W. Norton & Co. N.Y., 1971.

Hudson Roger, editor, *The Grand Quarrel*. Folio Society: London, 1993.

Jay, Peter, tr. *The Greek Anthology*. Penguin Books: 1981.

Latourette, K. S. *A History of Christianity*. Harper and Row. revised edition N.Y., 1975.

_____. *A History of the Expansion of Christianity*. Zondervan Publishing: Grand Rapids.

Living Doctrines of the New Testament. Pickering and Inglis Ltd., London, 1971.

Main, George F., tr. *The Imitation of Christ* (Thomas a Kempis). William Collins Sons & Co. Ltd., London, 1977.

Martin, Walter. *The Kingdom of the Cults*. Bethany Fellowship Inc., Minneapolis, Minnesota, 1977.

Metford, J. C., compiler, *Dictionary of Christian Law and Legend*. Thames and Hudson: London, 1983.

Muggeridge, Malcolm. *Jesus - The Man Who Lives*. Fontana/Collins: London, U.K., 1975.

New Bible Dictionary. The Intervarsity Fellowship: London, 1967.

Ogilvie, R. M. *The Age Of Augustus*. W.W. Norton & Co. Inc., 1975.

Price, R. M., tr. *Religious History* (Theodoret).

_____. tr. *A History of the Monks of Syria* (Theodoret). Cistercian Publications: Kalamazoo, Michigan, 1985.

Quiller-Crouch, Arthur, editor, *The Oxford Book of English Verse*. 1919.

Roberts, A. and J. Donaldson., editors, *The Ante-Nicene Nicene Fathers*. Eerdmann's Pub. Co. Grand Rapids, 1979.

Schaff, Philip. *History of the Church.*

Sirach, The Apocrypha

Stoner, P. W. and Newman, R. C. *Science Speaks. Moody Press: Chicago, 1976.*

Tobit, The Apocrypha

Twain, Mark. *The Prince and the Pauper.* (1882).

Warrington, John, tr. *Pensees* (Pascal). J.M. Dent & Sons Ltd., London, 1967.

Watling, E. F., tr. *Four Tragedies and Octavia*. Penguin Books: London, 1970.

Wirt, Sherwood E., tr. *The Confessions of Augustine*. Lion Publishing: Tring, Herts, U.K. 1971.

BIBLE COMMENTARIES

Anders, Max, editor. *Holman New Testament Commentary*. B & H Publishing Group: Nashville, Tennessee, 2004.

Barnes, Albert (1798-1870) *Notes on the Bible.*

Bible Background Commentary. Intervarsity Press: Nottingham, U.K., 1993.

Calvin, John (1509-1564). *Calvin's Commentaries.*

Clarke, Adam (1715-1832). *Commentary on the Bible.*

College Press NIV Commentary, The. Joplin, Missouri, 1996.

Excell, Joseph S. and Spence-Jones, H. D. M., editors, *The Pulpit Commentary.* 1881.

Gaebelein, Frank E., editor, *The Expositor's Bible Commentary*. Zondervan Publishers: Grand Rapids, Michigan.

Gill, John (1690-1771). *Exposition of the Entire Bible.*

Hawker, Robert. *The Poor Man's Commentary On The Whole Bible.* 1850.

Henry, Matthew. *Commentary On The Whole Bible.* Marshall, Morgan, and Scott: London, 1953

Hodge, Charles (1797-1878). *A Commentary on Ephesians.* Intervarsity Press.

Interpreter's Bible, The. Abingdon Press: New York, 1952.

Ironside, H. A. *Expository Commentary* (1876-1951).

IVP New Testament Commentary Series, The. Intervarsity Press: Nottingham, UK.

Jamieson R., A. Fausett, and D. Brown. *A Commentary on the Old and New Testaments,* 1871.

Johnson B. W. *The People's New Testament Commentary.* Word Search Corporation: Nashville, Tennessee, 2010

Macdonald, William. *The Believer's Bible Commentary.* Thomas Nelson Publishers: 1989.

Nelson's New Illustrated Bible Commentary. Thomas Nelson Inc., New York, 1999.

New Testament Commentary, The. Baker's Publishing House: Grand Rapids, Michigan, 1987.

Poole, Matthew. *Matthew Poole's Commentary.* 1685

Preacher's Commentary, The. Word Inc., Nashville, Tennessee, 1992.

Preacher's Outline and Sermon Bible. Word Search Corporation: Nashville, Tennessee, 2010.

Robertson A. T. *Word Pictures in the New Testament;* 1933.

Stern, David H. *Jewish New Testament Commentary.* Jewish New Testament Publications Inc., Clarksville, Maryland; 1982.

Trapp, John. *Commentary On The Old And New Testaments* (1601-1669).

Vincent, Marvin R. *Vincent's Word Studies*. 1886

Walvoord, John, and Zuck, Roy. *The Bible Knowledge Commentary*. Cook Communications: Colorado Springs, Colorado, 1989.

Wesley, John. *Explanatory Notes On The Whole Bible* (1703-1791).

Wiersbe, Warren W. *Wiersbe's Expository Outlines*. Pub. David C. Cook: Colorado Springs, Colorado

Wiseman, D. J. General editor. *Tyndale Old Testament Commentaries*. Intervarsity Press.

BIBLE VERSIONS

In addition to the *KJV* or *Authorised Version* of the Bible, the following versions or translations are cited, or were consulted by the author of this work.

CEV – *Contemporary English Version*; the American Bible Society, New York, NY; 1995.

ESV – *English Standard Version*; Crossway Bibles, a publishing ministry of Good News Publishers; Wheaton, Illinois; 2001.

GNB – *Good News Bible*; Second Edition, by the American Bible Society; New York, NY; 1992.

GW – *God's Word*; God's Word to the Nations Bible Society; Cleveland, Ohio; 1995.

JPS – *The JPS Bible*; the Jewish Publication Society; Philadelphia, PA; 1995.

ISV – *International Standard Version*, v. 1.2.2; The ISV Foundation, La Mirada, CA; 2001.

NET – *The Net Bible*; Biblical Studies Press; Richardson, Texas; 2006.

NIV – *New International Version*; Zondervan Bible Publishers, Grand Rapids, Michigan; 1978.

NJB – *New Jerusalem Bible*; Doubleday & Co. Inc; Garden City, New York; 1985

NRSV – *New Revised Standard Version*; the Division of Christian Education of the National Council of the Churches of Christ in the USA; 1989.

REB – *Revised English Bible with Apocrypha*; Oxford University Press; 1989.

YLT – *Young's Literal Translation*; by NJ Young; 1898.

250

www.ingramcontent.com/pod-product-compliance
Lightning Source LLC
Chambersburg PA
CBHW070524170426
43200CB00011B/2313